THE
Fat C

We know we eat more fat than is good for us, and we want to do something about it—which is why we use *The Fat Counter*. Now, with *THE POCKET FAT COUNTER*, we won't ever have to wonder how much fat is in an item at the supermarket or in a restaurant. *THE POCKET FAT COUNTER* makes it deliciously easy to live a healthy, lowfat lifestyle while keeping on the move.

ANNETTE B. NATOW, Ph.D., R.D., and JO-ANN HESLIN, M.A., R.D., are the authors of nineteen books on nutrition. Both are former faculty members of Adelphi University and the State University of New York, Downstate Medical Center. They are editors of the *Journal of Nutrition for the Elderly*, serve as editorial board members for the *Environmental Nutrition Newsletter*, and are frequent contributors to magazines and journals.

For orders other than by individual consumers, Pocket Books
grants a discount on the purchase of **10 or more** copies of
single titles for special markets or premium use. For further
details, please write to the Vice-President of Special Markets,
Pocket Books, 1633 Broadway, New York, NY 10019-6785,
8th Floor.

For information on how individual consumers can place
orders, please write to Mail Order Department, Simon &
Schuster Inc., 200 Old Tappan Road, Old Tappan, NJ 07675.

THE POCKET
FAT
COUNTER

ANNETTE B. NATOW, Ph.D.,R.D.,

and

JO-ANN HESLIN, M.A.,R.D.

POCKET BOOKS

New York   London   Toronto   Sydney   Tokyo   Singapore

An *Original* Publication of POCKET BOOKS

POCKET BOOKS, a division of Simon & Schuster Inc.
1230 Avenue of the Americas, New York, NY 10020

Copyright © 1996 by Jo-Ann Heslin and Annette Natow

ISBN: 0-671-53260-X

First Pocket Books printing May 1996

10 9 8 7 6 5 4 3 2 1

POCKET and colophon are registered trademarks of Simon & Schuster Inc.

Cover design by Tom McKeveny

Printed in the U.S.A.

To our families, who support us through every project: Harry, Allen, Irene, Sarah, Meryl, Laura, Marty, George, Emily, Steven, Joseph, Kristen and Karen

Acknowledgments

Without the tireless cooperation of Steven and Stephen, The Pocket Fat Counter would never have been completed. A special thanks to our editor, Julie Rubenstein, assistant editor Leslie Stern, and our agent, Nancy Trichter.

Our thanks also go to all the food manufacturers who graciously shared their data.

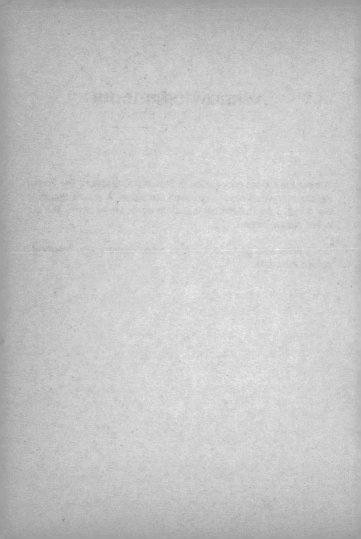

"Foods very high in fuel value, i.e., fats and dishes containing much fat, should be avoided."

Mary Swartz Rose, Ph.D.
Feeding the Family
The MacMillan Company, 1919

Sources of Data

Values in this counter have been obtained from the Composition of Foods, United States Department of Agriculture, Agricultural Handbooks: No. 8-1, Dairy and Egg Products; No. 8-2, Spices and Herbs; No. 8-3, Baby Foods; No. 8-4, Fats and Oils; No. 8-5, Poultry Products; No. 8-6, Soups, Sauces and Gravies; No. 8-7, Sausages and Luncheon Meats; No. 8-8, Breakfast Cereals; No. 8-9, Fruit and Fruit Juices; No. 8-10, Pork Products; No. 8-11, Vegetables and Vegetable Products; No. 8-12, Nut and Seed Products; No. 8-13, Beef Products; No. 8-14, Beverages; No. 8-15, Finfish and Shellfish Products; No. 8-16, Legumes and Legume Products; No. 8-17, Lamb, Veal and Game Products; No. 8-19, Snacks and Sweets; No. 8-20, Cereal Grains and Pasta; No. 8-21, Fast Foods; Supplements 1989, 1990, 1991, 1992.

Nutritive Value of Foods, United States Department of Agriculture, Home and Garden Bulletin No. 72.

J. Davies and J. Dickerson, *Nutrient Content of Food Portions*. Cambridge, UK: The Royal Society of Chemistry, 1991.

G. A. Leveille, M. E. Zabik, K. J. Morgan, *Nutrients in Foods*. Cambridge, MA: The Nutrition Guild, 1983.

Souci, Fachmann, Kraut, *Food Composition and Nutrition Tables*. Stuttgart: Wissenschaftliche Verlagsgesellschaft MbH, 1989.

Information from food labels, manufacturers and processors. The values are based on research conducted prior to 1995. Manufacturers' ingredients are subject to change, so current values may vary from those listed in the book.

INTRODUCTION

How can this book help me?

All the information you need about fat is in your pocket. The message is clear—eating less fat is better for you. Eating a lot of fat is not healthy. It causes most of the deaths in this country. Heart attacks, strokes, some cancers, diabetes, gallbladder disease, osteoarthritis and gout are some of the health problems caused or aggravated by high fat intake. And high-fat diets lead to overweight, which is a health risk by itself.

But don't I need some fat?

Yes, you do need a small amount of fat for good health, but you really can't avoid getting this small amount of fat. There is some fat—more or less—in almost all of the foods we eat.

Is it true that oils are good for me?

Foods that contain polyunsaturated and monounsaturated fats—oils, nuts, olives, fish—are better choices than foods high in saturated fat, like whole milk, cheese, butter, lunch meats and regular ice cream. Most saturated fat raises blood cholesterol levels, increasing the risk for heart attack. Research suggests that too much polyunsaturated fat may cause gallbladder disease and depress the immune system. While monounsaturated fat seems to be a healthier choice, it does contain the same amount of calories as any other fat, so it's not good to eat too much.

Once you have eaten a small amount of fat, there really is no benefit in having more. The best advice is to eat less fat. *The Pocket Fat Counter* will help you do this when you are on the move throughout your busy days. With *The Pocket Fat Counter* in your pocket or bag you'll never have to wonder about how much fat is in an item you are choosing in a restaurant or supermarket. You can still enjoy having your favorites and trying new dishes, if you follow some simple guidelines that won't take the fun out of eating.

One way to recognize foods high in fat is to look at the ingredient list. Lard, suet, chicken fat, butter, cocoa butter, cream, cheese, whole milk, diglycerides, fat, hydrogenated fat, hydrogenated oil, margarine, monoglycerides, oil, partially hydrogenated fat, partially hydrogenated oil, shortening, vegetable fat and vegetable oil are all fats.

TIPS TO LOWER FAT INTAKE WHEN EATING OUT

Have Food Naked

• Enjoy bread and rolls, but have them naked. Ask the waiter to take the butter away.

• Enjoy salad naked, minus regular dressing. Ask for lowfat or fat-free dressing, flavored vinegar or a squeeze of lemon.

• Enjoy a single burger, but hold the sauce, cheese and bacon. Dress it with lettuce, tomatoes, onions, pickles, ketchup or barbecue sauce.

• Enjoy pizza, but hold the extra cheese, sausage and pepperoni. Ask for peppers, onions or mushrooms instead.

• Enjoy baked or broiled fish. Ask for sauce on the side and some extra lemon wedges.

• Enjoy grilled or roast chicken. Remove the skin and hold the creamy dressing; use barbecue sauce, salsa or ketchup instead.

• Enjoy pasta with marinara, fresh tomato sauce or topped with vegetables. Skip the creamy white or meat sauces.

• Enjoy clear noodle or vegetable soup. Steer clear of cream soups or bisque.

- Enjoy pancakes with syrup, but hold the butter.
- Enjoy regular size muffins, and skip the butter.
- Enjoy your favorite pie. Eat the filling, leave the crust.
- Enjoy coffee or tea. Ask for milk instead of cream.

Paper napkins have lots of uses. Place a muffin or other pastry on one. If it leaves a grease ring, you'll know the pastry has lots of fat. You can also use a paper napkin to blot off the oil that often pools on top of pizza. Fries will give up some of their fat when placed on a paper napkin.

TIPS FOR BUYING LOWER-FAT FOODS

• Choose skim or lowfat milk, evaporated skim milk, and lowfat or nonfat yogurt. Look for these words: skim, 1% fat, 2% fat, fat-free, nonfat.

• Choose reduced-fat or fat-free cheeses. Those labeled part skim milk still may be fairly high in fat.

• Choose lean meats trimmed of all visible fat and ground meat labeled "lean" or "extra lean."

• Choose poultry without skin and ground poultry made with all white meat. Don't assume that sausage or lunch meat made with poultry is low in fat; check the label. The same is true of meat substitutes, which may not be low in fat.

• Choose lean fish like cod, scrod, haddock and halibut. When using fatty fish like salmon, bluefish or mackerel, remove the skin and all visible fat.

• Choose fruit butters, fruit preserves, jelly and honey to use as a spread instead of butter or margarine.

• Choose cooking sprays and butter flavor sprinkles to reduce and replace some of the oil and butter you use.

• Choose bagels, English muffins and raisin bread for lowfat snacks instead of regular sweet rolls and donuts.

• Choose dried fruits—raisins, apples, prunes, peaches, apricots—for fat-free snacks.

• Choose baked chips—potato and corn—instead of the usual fried versions.

• Choose pretzels or air-popped popcorn for a very lowfat snack.

• Choose hard candy, marshmallows, gum drops, candy corn, licorice or presweetened ready-to-eat cereals for a lowfat sweet treat.

TOP TEN FAT-FREE FAVORITES

Angelfood cake	Rice cakes
Jelly beans	Italian ices
Apple butter	Espresso
Romaine	Strawberries
Fruit nectar	Champagne

USING YOUR POCKET FAT COUNTER

This book lists the fat, saturated fat and calorie content of more than 1800 foods. With *The Pocket Fat Counter* in your pocket, it's easy to choose lowfat foods. Because of this book's size, you may not always find your favorite brands listed. You will find enough—a few typical brand names and non-branded samples—to make a good estimate of the fat content of your favorite brand.

All foods are listed alphabetically, A to Z. The generic (non-branded) listings are first, followed by a brand-name list. Many meat and fish entries are given in 3-ounce portions. They are equal in size to a deck of cards or a tape cassette.

When you need a bigger reference—one with counts for more than 19,000 foods—go to *The Fat Counter*, now in its third edition. We've included two blank pages in *The Pocket Fat Counter* so that you can add counts for other foods from *The Fat Counter*.

DEFINITIONS

as prep (as prepared): refers to food that has been prepared according to package directions

generic (non-branded foods): describes a food without a brand name

lean and fat: describes meat with some fat on its edges that is not cut away before cooking or poultry prepared with skin and fat as purchased

lean only: lean portion, trimmed of all visible fat

tr (trace): value used when a food contains less than one calorie or less than one gram of saturated fat or total fat.

ABBREVIATIONS

avg	=	average
diam	=	diameter
fl	=	fluid
frzn	=	frozen
g	=	gram
in	=	inch
lb	=	pound
lg	=	large
med	=	medium
mg	=	milligram
oz	=	ounce
pkg	=	package
prep	=	prepared
pt	=	pint
qt	=	quart
reg	=	regular
serv	=	serving
sm	=	small
sq	=	square
tbsp	=	tablespoon
tr	=	trace
tsp	=	teaspoon
w/	=	with
w/o	=	without

EQUIVALENT MEASURES

DRY

3 teaspoons	=	1 tablespoon
4 tablespoons	=	¼ cup
8 tablespoons	=	½ cup
12 tablespoons	=	¾ cup
16 tablespoons	=	1 cup
1000 milligrams	=	1 gram
28 grams	=	1 ounce
4 ounces	=	¼ pound
8 ounces	=	½ pound
12 ounces	=	¾ pound
16 ounces	=	1 pound

LIQUID

2 tablespoons	=	1 ounce
2 ounces	=	¼ cup
4 ounces	=	½ cup
6 ounces	=	¾ cup
8 ounces	=	1 cup
2 cups	=	1 pint
4 cups	=	1 quart

NOTES

ALL FAT AND SATURATED FAT VALUES OF FOODS ARE GIVEN IN GRAMS (G).

A DASH (—) INDICATES DATA NOT AVAILABLE.

Discrepancies in figures are due to rounding, product reformulation and re-evaluation.

If you are an average-weight, moderately active adult and want a quick benchmark for total fat grams each day, simply divide your weight in half.

Saturated fat should equal no more than 10% of your total fat.

For example: If you weigh 120 pounds, you should have no more than 60 grams of fat a day (120 ÷ 2) and less than one-third of this amount as saturated fat.

EXTRA FAT COUNTS

FOOD	PORTION	CALS.	SAT. FAT	TOTAL FAT

EXTRA FAT COUNTS

FOOD	PORTION	CALS.	SAT. FAT	TOTAL FAT

THE POCKET
FAT
COUNTER

FOOD	PORTION	CALS.	SAT. FAT	TOTAL FAT
ALFALFA				
sprouts	1 tbsp	1	tr	tr
ALMONDS				
oil roasted, salted	1 oz	174	2	16
ANCHOVY				
canned in oil	5	42	tr	2
APPLE				
apple	1	81	tr	tr
dried rings	10	155	tr	tr
APPLE JUICE				
frzn, as prep	1 cup	111	tr	tr
Minute Maid Box	8.45 fl oz	120	0	0
Minute Maid Frozen	8 fl oz	110	0	0
Tropicana Season's Best	8 fl oz	110	0	0
APPLESAUCE				
Mott's Fruit Snacks Sweetened	4 oz	90	0	0
APRICOT JUICE				
nectar	1 cup	141	tr	tr
APRICOTS				
apricots	3	51	tr	tr
dried halves	10	83	tr	tr
juice pack w/skin	3 halves	40	tr	tr
ARTICHOKE				
cooked	1 med (4 oz)	60	tr	tr
sunchoke, sliced	½ cup	57	0	tr
Birds Eye Deluxe Hearts	½ cup	30	0	0
S&W Hearts Marinated	½ cup	255	—	26
ARUGULA				
raw	½ cup	2	—	tr
ASPARAGUS				
canned spears	½ cup	24	tr	1
cooked	4 spears	14	tr	tr
Birds Eye Spears	½ cup	25	0	0
AVOCADO				
avocado	1	324	5	31

FOOD	PORTION	CALS.	SAT. FAT	TOTAL FAT
BACON				
cooked	3 strips	109	3	9
BACON SUBSTITUTES				
Bac-Os	2 tsp (5 g)	25	—	1
Louis Rich Turkey Bacon	1 slice (0.5 oz)	30	1	3
BAGEL				
plain	1 (3½ in)	195	tr	1
Lender's Plain frzn	1 (2 oz)	150	—	1
Sara Lee Plain frzn	1 (3 oz)	230	—	1
BAMBOO SHOOTS				
Empress Sliced	2 oz	14	0	0
BANANA				
banana chips	1 oz	147	8	10
fresh	1	105	tr	tr
BEAN SPROUTS				
fresh	½ cup	16	tr	tr
La Choy	⅔ cup	8	tr	tr
BEANS				
Brick Oven Baked Beans	½ cup	160	—	2
Campbell Pork & Beans In Tomato Sauce	½ can (8 oz)	200	—	3
Chi-Chi's Refried	½ cup (4.2 oz)	130	1	6
S&W Mixed Bean Salad Marinated	½ cup	90	—	1
Van Camp's Baked Beans Fat Free	½ cup (4.6 oz)	130	0	0
Van Camp's Vegetarian In Tomato Sauce	½ cup (4.6 oz)	110	0	1
BEEF				
bottom round lean & fat trim ¼ in Choice, braised	3 oz	241	6	15
brisket whole lean & fat trim ¼ in, braised	3 oz	327	11	27
corned beef brisket, cooked	3 oz	213	5	16
eye of round lean & fat trim ¼ in Choice, roasted	3 oz	205	5	12
flank lean & fat trim 0 in, broiled	3 oz	192	5	11
ground extra lean, broiled medium	3 oz	217	5	14

FOOD	PORTION	CALS.	SAT. FAT	TOTAL FAT
ground lean, broiled medium	3 oz	231	6	16
porterhouse steak lean & fat trim ¼ in Choice, broiled	3 oz	260	8	19
t-bone steak lean & fat trim ¼ in Choice, broiled	3 oz	253	7	18
tenderloin lean & fat trim ¼ in Choice, broiled	3 oz	259	7	19
top round lean & fat trim ¼ in Choice, braised	3 oz	221	4	11
Hormel Corned Beef canned	2 oz	120	3	7
Hormel Corned Beef Hash	1 cup (8.3 oz)	390	10	24
Hormel Dried Sliced	10 slices (1 oz)	50	1	2
Mary Kitchen Roast Beef Hash	1 can (7.5 oz)	348	9	21
Weight Watchers Deli Thin Oven Roasted Cured	5 slices (⅓ oz)	10	—	tr
BEEF DISHES				
irish stew	1 cup (7 oz)	280	9	16
roast beef sandwich, plain	1	346	4	14
roast beef submarine sandwich w/ tomato lettuce & mayonnaise	1	411	7	13
Dinty Moore American Classics Beef Stew	1 bowl (10 oz)	260	6	13
Hamburger Helper Beef Noodle, as prep	1 cup	330	—	15
Manwich Sloppy Joe as prep	1 sandwich	310	5	13
BEER AND ALE				
alcohol free beer	7 fl oz	50	—	tr
ale brown	10 oz	77	—	0
ale pale	10 oz	88	—	0
beer light	12 oz can	100	0	0
beer regular	12 oz can	146	0	0
BEETS				
sliced, cooked	½ cup (3 oz)	38	tr	tr
Seneca Pickled	2 tbsp	20	0	0
BISCUIT				
plain	1 (35 g)	276	9	34

FOOD	PORTION	CALS.	SAT. FAT	TOTAL FAT
w/ egg & bacon	1	457	10	31
w/ egg & sausage	1	582	15	39
Bisquick	½ cup (2 oz)	240	2	8
Bisquick Reduced Fat	½ cup (2 oz)	210	1	4
BLACKEYE PEAS				
dried, cooked	1 cup	198	tr	1
BLINTZE				
Empire Cheese	2 (4.4 oz)	200	2	6
BLUEBERRIES				
blueberries	1 cup	82	—	1
BLUEFISH				
baked	3 oz	135	1	5
BOK CHOY				
Dole, shredded	½ cup	5	—	tr
BRAN				
oat bran, cooked	½ cup	44	tr	tr
Kretschmer Toasted Wheat Bran	⅓ cup	57	tr	2
BRAZIL NUTS				
dried	1 oz	186	5	19
BREAD				
banana	1 slice (2 oz)	195	1	6
cornbread	2 in × 2 in (1.4 oz)	107	1	2
cracked wheat	1 slice	65	tr	1
naan	1 (6 oz)	571	—	21
sourdough	1 slice (1 oz)	78	tr	1
white, toasted	1 slice	67	tr	1
Arnold Cinnamon Raisin	1 slice (0.9 oz)	70	0	1
Arnold Pumpernickel	1 slice (1.1 oz)	70	0	1
Beefsteak Hearty Rye	1 slice (1 oz)	70	0	1
Dicarlo's Foccaccia	⅛ bread (2 oz)	130	0	2
Home Pride Wheat	1 slice (0.9 oz)	70	0	1
Sahara Pita White	½ pocket	78	—	1
Weight Watchers Italian	1 slice (0.8 oz)	38	tr	tr
Wonder 100% Whole Wheat	1 slice (1 oz)	70	0	1
Wonder French	1 slice (1 oz)	80	0	2
Wonder White	1 slice (0.9 oz)	70	0	1

FOOD	PORTION	CALS.	SAT. FAT	TOTAL FAT
BREADSTICKS				
Keebler Plain	2	30	tr	tr
BREAKFAST BAR				
Nutri-Grain Apple	1 (1.3 oz)	150	1	5
BREAKFAST DRINKS				
Carnation Instant Breakfast, Creamy Milk Chocolate	8 fl oz	220	2	3
Carnation Instant Breakfast, French Vanilla	1 pkg + skim milk	220	tr	1
Pillsbury Instant Breakfast, Chocolate, as prep w/ milk	1 serv	290	—	9
Pillsbury Instant Breakfast, Vanilla, as prep w/ milk	1 serv	300	—	9
BROCCOLI				
chopped, cooked	½ cup	22	tr	tr
raw	½ cup	12	tr	tr
Green Giant In Cheese Sauce	½ cup	60	tr	2
BROWNIE				
homemade w/ walnuts	1 (0.8 oz)	112	2	7
Little Debbie Fudge	1 pkg (2.1 oz)	270	3	13
Weight Watchers Chocolate Brownie	1 (1.25 oz)	100	tr	3
BRUSSELS SPROUTS				
cooked	½ cup	30	tr	tr
BULGUR				
cooked	½ cup	76	tr	tr
BUTTER				
butter	1 pat	36	3	4
Land O'Lakes whipped	1 tbsp (0.3 oz)	70	5	7
BUTTER BLENDS				
Touch of Butter Tub	1 tbsp	50	1	6
Country Morning Blend Land O'Lakes	1 tbsp	100	3	11
BUTTER SUBSTITUTES				
Molly McButter	½ tsp (1 g)	3	—	tr

FOOD	PORTION	CALS.	SAT. FAT	TOTAL FAT
CABBAGE				
coleslaw w/ dressing	½ cup	42	tr	2
green, shredded raw	½ cup (1.2 oz)	17	tr	tr
sweet & sour red cabbage	4 oz	61	—	3
CAKE				
angelfood	¹⁄₁₂ cake (1 oz)	73	0	0
baklava	1 oz	126	4	9
eclair	1 (1.4 oz)	149	—	10
sponge	¹⁄₁₂ cake (1.3 oz)	110	tr	1
tiramisu	1 piece (5.1 oz)	409	15	30
Drake's Coffee Cake	1 pkg (1.1 oz)	140	—	6
Drake's Devil Dog	1 (1.5 oz)	160	—	6
Drake's Ring Ding	1 (1.5 oz)	180	—	10
Entenmann's Coffee Cake Crumb	1 serv (1.3 oz)	160	—	7
Hostess Cup Cakes Chocolate	1 (1.6 oz)	170	3	5
Hostess Ding Dongs	1 (1.3 oz)	160	6	9
Hostess Ho Ho's	1 (1 oz)	130	4	6
Hostess Twinkies	1 (1.4 oz)	140	2	4
Pepperidge Farm Apple Turnover	1	300	—	17
Pepperidge Farm Classic Carrot	1 cake	260	6	16
Pop-Tarts Brown Sugar Cinnamon	1	210	2	8
Sara Lee All Butter Pound	1 slice (1 oz)	130	—	7
Sara Lee Cheesecake Original Plain	1 slice (2.8 oz)	230	—	11
Toast-R-Cakes Corn	1	120	—	4
Weight Watchers Chocolate	1 (2.5 oz)	180	tr	5
CALZONE				
cheese	1 (12 oz)	1020	24	54
CANADIAN BACON				
canadian bacon	2 slices (1.9 oz)	89	1	4
CANDY				
fudge chocolate	1 oz	115	2	3
jelly beans	1 oz	105	tr	tr
Almond Joy	1 (1.76 oz)	250	—	14
Baby Ruth Nestle	1 bar (2.1 oz)	280	7	12
Butterfinger Nestle	1 bar (2.1 oz)	280	6	11
Charms Pop	1 (0.6 oz)	70	0	0

FOOD	PORTION	CALS.	SAT. FAT	TOTAL FAT
Chuckles	4 pieces (1.4 oz)	140	0	0
Chunky Nestle	1 bar (1.4 oz)	200	6	11
Good & Plenty Snacksize	3 boxes (1.5 oz)	140	0	0
Gummy Bears Brock	5 pieces (1.4 oz)	130	0	0
Hershey Bar	1 (1.55 oz)	240	—	14
Hershey Bar With Almonds	1 (1.45 oz)	230	—	14
Hershey's Kisses	9 pieces (1.46 oz)	220	—	13
Kit Kat Wafer	1 (1.625 oz)	250	—	13
M&M's Peanut	1 pkg (1.7 oz)	250	5	13
M&M's Plain	1 pkg (1.7 oz)	230	10	10
Milky Way	1 bar (2.1 oz)	280	5	11
Mounds	1 (1.9 oz)	260	—	14
Pez	1 roll (0.3 oz)	35	0	0
Reese's Peanut Butter Cups	1 (1.8 oz)	280	—	17
Snickers	1 bar (2.1 oz)	280	5	14
Sno Caps Nestle	1 pkg (2.3 oz)	300	8	13
Starburst Tropical Fruits	8 pieces (1.4 oz)	160	1	3
3 Musketeers	1 (2.1 oz)	260	5	8
Tootsie Roll	1 (1 oz)	110	0	2
York Peppermint Patty	1 (1.5 oz)	180	—	4
CANTALOUPE				
half	½	94	—	1
CARROT JUICE				
canned	6 oz	73	tr	tr
CARROTS				
raw	1 (2.5 oz)	31	tr	tr
slices, canned	½ cup	17	tr	tr
slices, cooked frzn	½ cup	26	tr	tr
CASABA				
cubed	1 cup	45	—	tr
CASHEWS				
oil roasted, salted	1 oz	163	3	14
CATFISH				
channel, breaded & fried	3 oz	194	3	11
CATSUP				
Heinz	1 tbsp	16	0	0

FOOD	PORTION	CALS.	SAT. FAT	TOTAL FAT
CAULIFLOWER				
cooked	½ cup (2.2 oz)	14	tr	tr
flowerets raw	3 (2 oz)	14	tr	tr
Green Giant In Cheese Sauce	½ cup	60	tr	2
CAVIAR				
black granular	1 tbsp	40	—	3
CELERY				
raw	1 stalk (1.3 oz)	6	tr	tr
CEREAL				
corn grits, cooked	1 cup	146	tr	1
puffed rice	1 cup	57	—	tr
Cheerios	1¼ cup (1 oz)	110	—	2
Cocoa Puffs	1 cup (1 oz)	110	—	1
Froot Loops	1 cup (1 oz)	110	0	1
Frosted Flakes	¾ cup (1 oz)	110	0	0
Frosted Mini-Wheats	4 biscuits (1 oz)	100	0	0
Kellogg's All-Bran	⅓ cup (1 oz)	70	0	1
Kellogg's Bran Flakes	⅔ cup (1 oz)	90	0	tr
Kellogg's Corn Flakes	1 cup (1 oz)	100	0	0
Kix	1½ cup (1 oz)	110	—	1
Nabisco Cream of Wheat Quick	1 oz	100	tr	tr
Pillsbury Farina	⅔ cup	80	—	tr
Post Grape-Nuts	¼ cup (1 oz)	105	0	0
Post Raisin Bran	⅔ cup (40 g)	122	—	1
Product 19	1 cup (1 oz)	100	0	0
Quaker Oat Bran, cooked	⅓ cup	92	tr	2
Quaker Quick Oats	⅔ cup	99	tr	2
Rice Krispies	1 cup (1 oz)	110	0	0
Special K	1 cup (1 oz)	100	0	0
Sunbelt Muesli	1.9 oz	210	1	2
Total	1 cup (1 oz)	100	—	1
Wheatena	⅓ cup (1.4 oz)	150	0	1
Wheaties	1 cup (1 oz)	100	—	1
CHAMPAGNE				
Andre Brut	1 fl oz	21	0	0
Tott's Blanc de Noir	1 fl oz	22	0	0

FOOD	PORTION	CALS.	SAT. FAT	TOTAL FAT
CHEESE DISHES				
cheese omelette, as prep w/ 2 eggs	1 (6.8 oz)	519	—	44
macaroni & cheese	6.3 oz	320	—	19
CHEESE NATURAL				
bel paese	3½ oz	391	—	30
cheddar reduced fat	1.4 oz	104	—	6
emmentaler	3½ oz	403	—	30
goat semi-soft	1 oz	103	6	8
gorgonzola	3½ oz	376	—	31
port du salut	1 oz	100	5	8
roquefort	1 oz	105	5	9
yogurt cheese	1 oz	20	—	0
Alpine Lace Havarti Reduced Fat	1 piece (1 oz)	90	5	25
Alpine Lace Provolone Reduced Fat	1 piece (1 oz)	70	3	5
Bresse Brie	1 oz	110	5	9
Cabot Monterey Jack	1 oz	80	5	5
Casino Havarti	1 oz	120	7	11
Casino Romano Grated	1 oz	130	6	9
Churney Feta	1 oz	80	4	6
Dorman Colby	1 oz	110	—	9
Dorman Muenster	1 oz	110	—	9
Friendship Farmer	2 tbsp (1 oz)	50	2	3
Friendship Hoop	2 tbsp (1 oz)	20	0	0
Frigo Asiago	1 oz	110	—	9
Frigo Parmesan Dry Grated	1 oz	130	—	9
Frigo String	1 oz	80	—	5
Heluva Good Cheese Mozzarella Part Skim Low Moisture Shredded	¼ cup (1 oz)	80	3	5
Heluva Good Cheese Mozzarella Whole Milk	1 oz	80	4	6
Heluva Good Cheese Swiss	1 oz	112	5	8
Hollow Road Farms Sheep's Milk	1 oz	45	—	3
Kraft Cheddar	1 oz	110	5	9

FOOD	PORTION	CALS.	SAT. FAT	TOTAL FAT
Kraft Provolone	1 oz	100	4	7
Land O'Lakes Brick	1 oz	100	5	8
Land O'Lakes Swiss Light	1 oz	80	3	4
Laughing Cow Babybel	1 oz	90	5	7
Marin French Cheese Camembert	1 oz	86	4	7
Polly-O Mozzarella Free	1 oz	35	0	0
Polly-O Ricotta Free	¼ cup	50	0	0
Polly-O Ricotta Part Skim	¼ cup	90	4	6
Polly-O Ricotta Whole Milk	¼ cup	110	5	8
Sargento Blue	1 oz	100	—	8
Sargento Edam	1 oz	101	—	8
Sargento Fontina	1 oz	110	—	9
Sargento Gjetost	1 oz	132	—	8
Sargento Jarlsberg	1 oz	100	—	7
Sargento Limburger	1 oz	93	—	8
Weight Watchers Mozzarella	1 oz	70	3	4
CHEESE PROCESSED				
Alouette Garlic	2 tbsp (0.8 oz)	70	5	7
Alouette Light Garlic Alouette	2 tbsp (0.8 oz)	50	3	4
Borden American Slices	1 oz	110	5	9
Cheez Whiz	1 oz	80	3	6
Cracker Barrel Port Wine Cheddar	1 oz	100	4	7
Healthy Choice Yellow Singles Fat Free	1 slice (0.67 oz)	25	0	0
Lactaid American	3.5 oz	328	15	25
Laughing Cow Cheesebits	6 pieces (1 oz)	70	4	6
Light N' Lively Singles American	1 oz	70	3	4
Rondele Soft Spreadable Garlic & Herbs	2 tbsp (1 oz)	100	6	9
Smart Beat American	1 slice (0.6 oz)	35	1	2
Spreadery Mild Mexican With Jalapeno Peppers	1 oz	70	3	4
Squeez-A-Snak Sharp	1 oz	80	4	7
Velveeta Slices	1 oz	90	4	6
Weight Watchers American Slices Yellow	2 slices (⅔ oz)	35	1	1

FOOD	PORTION	CALS.	SAT. FAT	TOTAL FAT
CHEESE SUBSTITUTES				
Golden Image American	1 oz	90	2	6
CHERRIES				
sweet fresh	10	49	tr	1
CHESTNUTS				
cooked	1 oz	37	tr	tr
CHEWING GUM				
Chiclets	1 piece (1.59 g)	6	0	0
Dentyne	1 piece (1.88 g)	6	0	0
Juicy Fruit	1 stick	10	—	tr
CHICKEN				
boneless breaded & fried w/ barbecue sauce	6 pieces (4.6 oz)	330	6	18
boneless breaded & fried w/ sweet & sour sauce	6 pieces (4.6 oz)	346	6	18
broiler/fryer breast w/ skin, batter dipped & fried	2.9 oz	218	3	11
broiler/fryer breast w/ skin, roasted	½ breast (3.4 oz)	193	2	8
broiler/fryer breast w/o skin, roasted	½ breast (3 oz)	142	1	3
broiler/fryer drumstick w/ skin, batter dipped & fried	1 (2.6 oz)	193	3	11
broiler/fryer drumstick w/ skin, roasted	1 (1.8 oz)	112	2	6
broiler/fryer drumstick w/o skin, roasted	1 (1.5 oz)	76	1	2
roaster light meat w/o skin, roasted	1 cup (5 oz)	214	2	6
Banquet Boneless Chicken Nuggets	2.5 oz	200	—	13
Banquet Fried Chicken Breast Portions	5.75 oz	220	—	11
Carl Buddig	1 oz	50	2	3
Country Skillet Chicken Patties	3 oz	230	—	15

FOOD	PORTION	CALS.	SAT. FAT	TOTAL FAT
Healthy Choice Breast Oven Roasted	1.9 oz	60	1	2
Hillshire Lunch 'N Munch Smoked Chicken/Monterey/Snickers	1 pkg (4.25 oz)	400	—	23
Swanson Thighs And Drumsticks	3¼ oz	290	—	18
Tyson Microwave Breast Sandwich	4.25 oz	328	—	14
Weaver Batter Dipped Wings	4 oz	400	—	28
Weaver Hot Wings	2.7 oz	170	—	11
Weaver Rondelets Cheese	1 (2.6 oz)	190	—	11
Weight Watchers Roasted Chicken Ham	2 slices (¾ oz)	25	—	1

CHICKEN DISHES

FOOD	PORTION	CALS.	SAT. FAT	TOTAL FAT
cacciatore	¾ cup	394	6	24
chicken & dumplings	¾ cup	256	4	12
sandwich fillet plain	1	515	9	29
sandwich fillet w/ cheese, lettuce, mayonnaise & tomato	1	632	12	39
Dinty Moore American Classics Chicken & Noodles	1 bowl (10 oz)	260	4	8

CHICKEN SUBSTITUTES

FOOD	PORTION	CALS.	SAT. FAT	TOTAL FAT
LaLoma Chik Nuggets	5 nuggets (85 g)	270	—	20
White Wave Meatless Sandwich Slices	2 slices (1.6 oz)	80	0	0

CHICKPEAS

FOOD	PORTION	CALS.	SAT. FAT	TOTAL FAT
canned	1 cup	285	tr	3

CHILI

FOOD	PORTION	CALS.	SAT. FAT	TOTAL FAT
con carne w/ beans	8.9 oz	254	3	8
Chi-Chi's San Antonio	1 cup (8.5 oz)	240	1	19
Health Valley Spicy Vegetarian With Beans	5 oz	160	—	4
Hormel Chili No Beans	1 cup (8.3 oz)	410	13	30
Old El Paso Chili Con Carne	1 cup	162	—	7

CHIPS

FOOD	PORTION	CALS.	SAT. FAT	TOTAL FAT
corn puffs cheese	1 oz	157	2	10
potato sticks	1 pkg (1 oz)	148	3	10
Cape Cod Potato Chips	19 chips (1 oz)	150	2	8

FOOD	PORTION	CALS.	SAT. FAT	TOTAL FAT
Eagle Tortilla Chips	1 oz	150	—	8
Fritos Corn Chips	34 pieces (1 oz)	150	—	10
Guiltless Gourmet Baked Tortilla Chips	22–26 chips (1 oz)	110	—	1
Health Valley Country Ripple No Salt Added	1 oz	160	—	10
Lay's Potato Sour Cream & Onion	17 pieces (1 oz)	160	—	10
Louise's Low-Fat Nacho Cheese Tortilla Chips	30 chips (1 oz)	130	1	3
Louise's Potato Fat-Free	30 chips (1 oz)	110	0	0
Mr. Phipps Tater Crisps Original	11 (0.5 oz)	60	tr	2
Old El Paso Crispy Tortilla Corn Chips	16 chips (1 oz)	150	—	8
Pringles BBQ	14 chips (1 oz)	150	3	10
Pringles Right BBQ Pringles	16 chips (1 oz)	140	2	7
Sunchips	12 pieces (1 oz)	150	—	8
Weight Watchers Corn Snacker	½ oz	60	—	2
Weight Watchers Great Snackers Cheddar Cheese	½ oz	70	1	3
Wise Natural Potato Chips	1 oz	160	—	11
CHOCOLATE				
powder, as prep w/ whole milk	9 oz	226	5	9
Baker's Semi-Sweet Chips	¼ cup	197	—	9
Hershey Semi-Sweet Chips	¼ cup (1.5 oz)	220	—	12
Hershey's Syrup	2 tbsp	80	—	1
CILANTRO				
fresh	¼ cup	1	—	tr
CLAM JUICE				
Doxsee	3 fl oz	4	0	0
CLAMS				
breaded & fried	¾ cup	451	7	26
fresh, cooked	20 sm	133	tr	2
fresh, raw	9 lg (180 g)	133	tr	2
Doxsee Chopped	6.5 oz	90	—	tr
Mrs. Paul's Fried	2½ oz	200	—	9

FOOD	PORTION	CALS.	SAT. FAT	TOTAL FAT
Progresso Red Clam Sauce	½ cup	70	—	3
Progresso White Clam Sauce	½ cup	110	—	8
COCOA				
Nestle Hot Cocoa Mix With Marshmallows, as prep w/ skim milk	6 oz	190	—	1
Nestle Hot Cocoa Mix, as prep w/ whole milk	6 oz	230	—	8
Swiss Miss Cocoa Lite, as prep	6 oz	70	—	tr
COCONUT				
fresh	1 piece (1½ oz)	159	13	15
Baker's Premium Shred	⅓ cup	135	—	9
Coco Lopez Cream of Coconut	2 tbsp	120	—	5
COD				
dried	3 oz	246	tr	2
fresh cooked	1 fillet (6.3 oz)	189	tr	2
COFFEE				
brewed	6 oz	4	0	0
cafe au lait	1 cup (8 fl oz)	77	3	4
cappuccino mix, as prep	7 oz	62	2	2
capuccino	1 cup (8 fl oz)	77	3	4
expresso	1 cup (3 fl oz)	2	0	0
instant decaffeinated, as prep	6 oz	4	0	0
instant regular, as prep	6 oz	4	0	0
mocha	1 mug (9.6 fl oz)	202	9	15
mocha mix, as prep	7 oz	51	2	2
Kava Instant	1 tsp	2	0	0
COFFEE SUBSTITUTES				
Postum Instant	6 oz	11	0	0
COFFEE WHITENERS				
Cremora	1 tsp	12	—	1
Coffee-Mate Coffee-Nate	1 tbsp (0.5 fl oz)	16	tr	1
Naturally Yours International Delight Amaretto	1 tbsp (0.6 fl oz)	45	0	2
COLLARDS				
fresh, cooked	½ cup	17	—	tr

FOOD	PORTION	CALS.	SAT. FAT	TOTAL FAT
COOKIES				
chocolate chip lowfat	1 (0.25 oz)	45	tr	2
ladyfingers	1 (0.38 oz)	40	tr	1
molasses	1 (0.5 oz)	65	tr	2
peanut butter sandwich	1 (0.5 oz)	67	1	3
Archway Chocolate Chip	1 (1 oz)	130	2	6
Archway Coconut Macaroon	1 (0.8 oz)	90	4	5
Archway Pfeffernusse	2 (1.3 oz)	140	0	1
Bakery Wagon Ginger Snaps	5	160	2	7
Drake's Oatmeal	2 (1 oz)	120	—	5
Grandma's Peanut Butter	2 (2.75 oz)	410	—	30
Health Valley Honey Graham	7	100	—	4
La Choy Fortune Cookies	1	15	—	tr
Mother's Sugar	2	140	2	6
Nabisco Apple Newtons Fat Free	1 (0.75 oz)	70	0	0
Nabisco Brown Edge Wafers	2½ (0.5 oz)	70	tr	2
Nabisco Chips Ahoy! Real Chocolate Chip	1 (0.5 oz)	50	tr	2
Nabisco Fig Newtons	1 (0.5 oz)	60	tr	1
Nabisco Fig Newtons Fat Free	1 (0.75 oz)	70	0	0
Nabisco Lorna Doone	2 (0.5 oz)	70	tr	4
Nabisco Mallomars	1 (0.5 oz)	60	1	3
Nabisco Nilla Wafers	3½ (0.5 oz)	60	tr	2
Nabisco Oreo	1 (0.5 oz)	50	tr	2
Nabisco Social Tea	3 (0.5 oz)	70	tr	2
Snackwell's Devil's Food Cakes	1 (0.5 oz)	60	0	0
Stella D'Oro Kichel Low Sodium	21	150	—	9
Sunshine Animal Crackers	1 box (2 oz)	000	2	7
Sunshine Chip-A-Roos	3 (1.3 oz)	190	4	10
Sunshine Golden Fruit Raisin	1 (0.7 oz)	80	0	2
Sunshine Hydrox	3	150	2	7
Weight Watchers Chocolate	3	80	—	3
CORN				
fritters	1 (1 oz)	62	tr	2
on-the-cob w/ butter, cooked	1 ear	155	2	3
Birds Eye In Butter Sauce	½ cup	90	1	2

FOOD	PORTION	CALS.	SAT. FAT	TOTAL FAT
Green Giant	½ cup	70	0	0
Green Giant Mexi Corn	½ cup	80	—	tr
S&W Cream Style Homestyle	½ cup	105	—	1
CORNMEAL				
corn grits, cooked	1 cup	146	tr	tr
COTTAGE CHEESE				
Axelrod Nonfat	½ cup (4.4 oz)	90	0	0
Borden 4%	½ cup	120	—	5
Breakstone 2%	4 oz	100	1	2
Friendship Lowfat 1%	½ cup (4 oz)	90	1	1
Knudsen 2% With Pineapple	6 oz	170	2	2
Lactaid 1%	4 oz	72	1	1
Sargento Pot Cheese	1 oz	26	—	tr
COUGH DROPS				
Halls	1 (3.8 g)	15	0	0
COUSCOUS				
cooked	½ cup	101	tr	tr
CRAB				
alaska king, cooked	1 leg (4.7 oz)	129	tr	2
crab cakes	1 cake (2.1 oz)	93	1	5
soft-shell, fried	1 (4.4 oz)	334	4	18
S&W Dungeness Crab	3.25 oz	81	—	2
CRACKERS				
Better Cheddars	10 (0.5 oz)	70	tr	4
Cheez-It	27 (1 oz)	160	2	8
Cheez-It Reduced Fat	30 (1 oz)	130	1	5
Devonsheer Melba Rounds Plain	½ oz	53	—	1
Hi Ho	9	160	2	9
Ideal Crispbread Extra Thin	3	48	0	0
Lance Oyster Crackers	1 pkg (14 g)	70	1	2
Little Debbie Cheese Crackers With Peanut Butter	1 pkg (1.4 oz)	210	3	10
Pepperidge Farm Goldfish Cheddar Cheese	1 pkg (1.5 oz)	190	2	6
Premium Saltine	5 (0.5 oz)	60	tr	2
Premium Saltine Fat Free	5 (0.5 oz)	50	0	0

FOOD	PORTION	CALS.	SAT. FAT	TOTAL FAT
Ritz	4 (0.5 oz)	70	tr	4
Rykrisp Natural	2	40	0	0
Ryvita Crisp Bread Dark Finn Crisp	2	38	—	tr
Snackwell's Cheese	18 (0.5 oz)	60	tr	1
Snackwell's Wheat	5 (0.5 oz)	50	0	0
Triscuit	3 (0.5 oz)	60	tr	2
Vegetable Thins	6 (0.5 oz)	70	tr	4
Wheatsworth Stone Ground	4 (0.5 oz)	70	tr	3
Zwieback	2 (0.5 oz)	60	tr	1

CRANBERRIES

FOOD	PORTION	CALS.	SAT. FAT	TOTAL FAT
Ocean Spray Cranberry Sauce Jellied	2 oz	90	0	0
Ocean Spray Cranberry Sauce Old Fashion Whole Berry S&W	½ cup	90	0	0

CRANBERRY JUICE

FOOD	PORTION	CALS.	SAT. FAT	TOTAL FAT
Apple & Eve	6 fl oz	100	0	0
Ocean Spray Cocktail	8 fl oz	140	0	0
Ocean Spray Cocktail Reduced Calorie	8 fl oz	50	0	0

CRAYFISH

FOOD	PORTION	CALS.	SAT. FAT	TOTAL FAT
cooked	3 oz	97	tr	1

CREAM

FOOD	PORTION	CALS.	SAT. FAT	TOTAL FAT
half & half	1 tbsp	20	1	2
whipped heavy cream	1 cup	411	55	44
Farmland Light Cream	2 tbsp	30	2	3

CREAM CHEESE

FOOD	PORTION	CALS.	SAT. FAT	TOTAL FAT
Alpine Lace Fat Free Garden Vegetable	2 tbsp (1 oz)	30	tr	tr
Fleur De Lait	2 tbsp (1 oz)	100	6	10
Friendship NY Style Reduced Fat	2 tbsp (1 oz)	50	2	3
Healthy Choice Fat Free	1 oz	25	0	0
Philadelphia Brand	1 oz	100	6	10
Philadelphia Brand Light	1 oz	60	3	5

CREAM CHEESE SUBSTITUTES

FOOD	PORTION	CALS.	SAT. FAT	TOTAL FAT
Tofutti Better Than Cream Cheese Plain	1 oz	80	2	8

FOOD	PORTION	CALS.	SAT. FAT	TOTAL FAT
CROISSANT				
plain	1	232	7	12
w/ egg, cheese & bacon	1	413	15	28
w/ egg, cheese & sausage	1	524	18	38
CROUTONS				
Pepperidge Farm Seasoned	½ oz	70	1	3
CUCUMBER				
cucumber salad	3.5 oz	50	tr	tr
raw	1 (11 oz)	38	tr	tr
CUSTARD				
baked	1 cup	305	7	17
zabaione	½ cup (57.2 g)	135	2	5
DANDELION GREENS				
fresh, cooked	½ cup	17	—	tr
DANISH PASTRY				
cinnamon	1 (4¼ in diam) (2.3 oz)	262	4	15
Pepperidge Farm Apple	1	220	—	8
Sara Lee Cheese	1	130	—	8
DATES				
dried whole	10	228	—	tr
DINNER FROZEN				
Armour Classics Chicken Parmigiana	11.5 oz	370	—	19
Armour Classics Meat Loaf	11.25 oz	360	—	17
Banquet Beans & Frankfurters Dinner	10 oz	350	—	14
Banquet Extra Helping Fried Chicken Dinner	14.25 oz	790	—	43
Budget Gourmet Beef Cantonese	1 pkg (9.1 oz)	270	—	9
Budget Gourmet Pepper Steak With Rice	1 pkg (10 oz)	300	—	8
Budget Gourmet Stuffed Turkey Breast	1 pkg (11 oz)	250	2	6
Healthy Choice Classics Mesquite Beef Barbecue	1 meal (11 oz)	310	2	4

FOOD	PORTION	CALS.	SAT. FAT	TOTAL FAT
Healthy Choice Classics Shrimp And Vegetables Maria	1 meal (12.5 oz)	260	1	2
Lean Cuisine Chicken Italiano	1 pkg (9 oz)	270	2	6
Lean Cuisine Fish Divan	1 pkg (10.4 oz)	210	1	6
Lean Cuisine Stuffed Cabbage	1 pkg (9.5 oz)	220	2	7
Le Menu LightStyle Sliced Turkey	10 oz	210	—	5
Le Menu LightStyle Veal Marsala	10 oz	230	—	3
Morton Gravy & Charbroiled Beef Patty	9 oz	270	—	12
Stouffer's Chicken A La King	1 pkg (9.5 oz)	320	3	10
Stouffer's Lunch Express Mandarin Chicken	1 pkg (9.75 oz)	270	1	6
Stouffer's Stuffed Pepper	1 pkg (10 oz)	200	2	8
Swanson Fish 'n' Chips	10 oz	500	—	21
Swanson Homestyle Seafood Creole With Rice	9 oz	240	—	6
Swanson Loin of Pork	10¾ oz	280	—	12
Tyson Healthy Portions BBQ Chicken	1 pkg (12.5 oz)	400	—	8
Ultra Slim-Fast Chicken Fettucini	12 oz	380	—	12
Ultra Slim-Fast Shrimp Marinara	12 oz	290	—	3
Weight Watchers Beef Sirloin Tips	7.5 oz	210	3	6
Weight Watchers Oven Baked Fish	7 oz	150	1	4
DIP				
Breakstone Clam	2 tbsp	50	3	4
Chi-Chi's Fiesta Bean	2 tbsp (0.9 oz)	35	1	2
Heluva Good Cheese French Onion	2 tbsp (1.1 oz)	50	3	5
Heluva Good Cheese French Onion Light	2 tbsp (1.1 oz)	35	1	2
Kraft Avocado Guacamole	2 tbsp	50	2	4
Wise Jalapeno Bean	2 tbsp	25	0	0
DOUGHNUTS				
creme filled	1 (3 oz)	307	6	21
french crueller glazed	1 (1.4 oz)	169	2	8
jelly	1 (3 oz)	289	4	16

FOOD	PORTION	CALS.	SAT. FAT	TOTAL FAT
Dutch Mill Donut Holes Double-Dipped Chocolate	3 (1.4 oz)	220	6	16
Hostess Crumb	1 (1 oz)	130	4	8
Hostess Old Fashioned Glazed	1 (2.1 oz)	250	5	12
Tastykake Powdered Sugar	1 (46 g)	180	2	9
DUCK				
w/ skin, roasted	½ duck (13.4 oz)	1287	37	108
w/o skin, roasted	½ duck (7.8 oz)	445	9	25
EDITIT				
domestic w/o bone, roasted	3 oz	167	2	7
EEL				
cooked	1 fillet (5.6 oz)	375	5	24
EGG				
fried w/ margarine	1	91	2	7
hard cooked	1	77	2	5
poached	1	74	2	5
scrambled plain	2	200	6	15
scrambled w/ whole milk & margarine	1	101	2	7
EGG DISHES				
deviled	2 halves	145	3	13
salad	½ cup	307	6	28
sandwich w/ cheese & ham	1	348	7	16
EGG SUBSTITUTES				
Egg Beaters Cheese Omelette	½ cup	110	2	5
Egg Watchers	2 oz	50	—	2
EGGNOG				
eggnog	1 cup	342	11	19
Borden Light	½ cup	130	—	2
EGGPLANT				
baba ghannouj	¼ cup	55	—	4
slices, cooked	4 (7 oz)	38	0	0
Mrs. Paul's Parmigiana	5 oz	240	—	16
ENDIVE				
raw, chopped	½ cup	4	tr	tr

FOOD	PORTION	CALS.	SAT. FAT	TOTAL FAT
ENGLISH MUFFIN				
plain, toasted	1	133	tr	1
w/ butter	1	189	2	6
Thomas'	1	130	—	1
Thomas' Sandwich Size	1 (92 g)	210	1	2
FALAFEL				
falafel	3 (1.8 oz)	170	1	9
FENNEL				
fresh, sliced	1 cup	27	—	tr
FIGS				
dried whole	10	477	tr	2
fresh	1 med	50	tr	tr
FILBERTS				
oil roasted	1 oz	187	1	18
FISH				
fish cake	1 (4.7 oz)	166	2	7
sandwich w/ tartar sauce	1	431	5	55
sticks	1 stick (1 oz)	76	1	3
taramasalata	3.5 oz	446	—	46
FLOUNDER				
fresh, cooked	3 oz	99	tr	1
Gorton's Fishmarket Fresh	5 oz	110	—	1
Mrs. Paul's Crunchy Batter Fillets	2 fillets	220	—	9
FRENCH TOAST				
w/ butter	2 slices	356	8	19
Aunt Jemima frzn	1 serv (3 oz)	166	1	4
Downyflake frzn	2	270	—	12
FRUIT DRINKS				
fruit punch, as prep w/water	1 cup	113	tr	tr
Boku White Grape Raspberry	1 bottle (16 fl oz)	120	0	0
Crystal Geyser Juice Squeeze Citrus Grape	1 bottle (12 fl oz)	145	0	0
Dole Pineapple Orange	6 fl oz	90	0	0
Juicy Juice Punch	1 box (8.45 fl oz)	140	0	0
Kern's Tropical Nectar	6 fl oz	110	0	0

FOOD	PORTION	CALS.	SAT. FAT	TOTAL FAT
Kool-Aid Mix Rainbow Punch, as prep	8 oz	98	0	0
Mauna La'i Mango & Hawaiian Guava Fruit Juice Drink	8 fl oz	130	0	0
Minute Maid Berry Punch	8 fl oz	130	0	0
Minute Maid Limeade	8 fl oz	100	0	0
Ocean Spray Cran. Grape	8 fl oz	170	0	0
Odwalla Guanaba Dabba Doo!	8 fl oz	130	0	0
Odwalla Mo Beta	16 fl oz	280	—	1
Sunny Delight	6 fl oz	90	0	0
Tropicana Twister Orange Peach	8 fl oz	120	0	0
FRUIT MIXED				
fruit cocktail in heavy syrup	½ cup	93	tr	tr
fruit cocktail juice pack	½ cup	56	tr	tr
Big Valley Cup A Fruit frzn	1 pkg (4 oz)	50	0	0
Hunt's Fruit Cocktail	4 oz	90	—	tr
S&W Fruit Cocktail Diet	½ cup	40	0	0
FRUIT SNACKS				
fruit leather rolls	1 sm (0.5 oz)	49	tr	tr
Fruit By The Foot Cherry	1	80	—	2
Fruit Roll-Ups Fruit Punch	1 (½ oz)	50	—	tr
Weight Watchers Cinnamon	½ oz	50	0	tr
GARLIC				
clove	1	4	tr	tr
GEFILTE FISH				
Manischewitz Sweet	1 piece	132	—	4
GELATIN				
fruit flavored, as prep	½ cup	70	0	0
low calorie, as prep	½ cup	8	0	0
GOAT				
roasted	3 oz	122	1	3
GOOSE				
w/ skin, roasted	6.6 oz	574	13	41
w/o skin, roasted	5 oz	340	7	18
GRANOLA				
Fi-Bar Coconut	1 bar	120	1	4

FOOD	PORTION	CALS.	SAT. FAT	TOTAL FAT
Hershey Chocolate Covered				
Cookies & Creme	1 bar (1.2 oz)	170	—	8
Kellogg's Low Fat	⅓ cup (1 oz)	110	0	2
Kudos Peanut Butter	1 bar (1 oz)	130	3	5
Nature Valley Cinnamon & Raisin	⅓ cup (1 oz)	120	—	4
Post Hearty	¼ cup (1 oz)	128	—	4
Quaker Chewy Chunky Nut &				
Raisin	1 bar	131	1	6
GRAPE JUICE				
Hi-C	8 fl oz	130	0	0
Juicy Juice	1 box	130	0	0
Minute Maid Chilled	8 fl oz	130	0	0
Tropicana Season's Best	8 fl oz	160	0	0
GRAPEFRUIT				
juice pack	½ cup	46	tr	tr
pink	½	37	tr	tr
red	½	37	tr	tr
white	½	39	tr	tr
S&W Sections Unsweetened	½ cup	40	0	0
S&W Sections In Light Syrup	½ cup	80	0	0
GRAPEFRUIT JUICE				
fresh	1 cup	96	tr	tr
Minute Maid frzn	8 fl oz	100	0	0
Tropicana	1 container (6 fl oz)	80	0	0
Tropicana Twister Pink	8 fl oz	110	0	0
GRAPES				
fresh	10	36	tr	tr
GRAVY				
beef	½ cup	35	tr	1
Franco-American Au Jus	2 oz	10	—	0
Franco-American Chicken	2 oz	45	—	4
Franco-American Mushroom	2 oz	25	—	1
Franco-American Turkey	2 oz	30	—	2
Gravymaster	¼ tsp	3	0	0
GREAT NORTHERN BEANS				
canned	1 cup	300	tr	1

FOOD	PORTION	CALS.	SAT. FAT	TOTAL FAT
dried, cooked	1 cup	210	tr	1
GREEN BEANS				
fresh, cooked	½ cup	25	0	0
Allen Italian	½ cup (4.2 oz)	35	0	1
Green Giant Cut In Butter Sauce	½ cup	30	tr	1
GUANABANA JUICE				
Libby Nectar	1 can (11.5 fl oz)	210	0	0
GUAVA				
fresh	1	45	tr	1
GUAVA JUICE				
Kern's Nectar	6 fl oz	110	0	0
HADDOCK				
cooked	1 fillet (5.3 oz)	168	tr	1
Gorton's Fishmarket Fresh	5 oz	110	—	1
Van De Kamp's Battered	2 pieces	250	3	15
HALIBUT				
cooked	3 oz	119	tr	2
Van De Kamp's Battered	2 pieces	150	1	6
HAM				
canned extra lean	3 oz	142	—	7
whole lean only, roasted	3 oz	133	2	5
Alpine Lace Boneless Cooked	2 slices (2 oz)	60	1	2
Armour Star Boneless	1 oz	41	—	2
Carl Buddig	1 oz	50	1	3
Hansel 'n Gretel Baked Virginia	1 oz	34	—	1
Healthy Choice Cooked	3 slices (2.2 oz)	70	1	2
Hormel Ham & Cheese Patties	1 patty (2 oz)	190	6	17
Hormel Spam Spread	4 tbsp (2 oz)	100	4	11
Krakus	1 oz	25	—	1
Louis Rich Carving Board Baked With Natural Juices	2 slices (1.6 oz)	45	0	1
Oscar Mayer Deli-Thin Honey Ham	4 slices (1.8 oz)	60	1	2
Oscar Mayer Dinner Slice	3 oz	90	1	3
Oscar Mayer Ham And Cheese Loaf	1 slice (1 oz)	70	3	5

FOOD	PORTION	CALS.	SAT. FAT	TOTAL FAT
Oscar Mayer Healthy Favorites Honey Ham	4 slices (1.8 oz)	50	1	2
Oscar Mayer Lunchables Cookies/ Ham/Swiss	1 pkg (4.2 oz)	360	8	19
Russer Baked	2 oz	70	1	3
Underwood Deviled	2.08 oz	220	6	19
Underwood Deviled Light	2.08 oz	120	1	8
Weight Watchers Deli Thin Oven Roasted	5 slices (⅓ oz)	12	—	tr
HAM DISHES				
croquettes	1 (3.1 oz)	217	5	14
salad	½ cup	287	5	23
sandwich w/ cheese	1	353	6	15
HAMBURGER				
double patty w/ bun	1 reg	544	10	28
double patty w/ cheese & double bun	1 reg	461	10	22
single patty w/ bun	1 lg	400	8	23
single patty w/ cheese & bun	1 lg	608	15	33
triple patty w/ cheese & bun	1 lg	769	22	51
Kid Cuisine Beef Patty Sandwich/ Cheese	6.25 oz	430	—	22
MicroMagic Cheeseburger	1 pkg (4.75 oz)	450	—	25
White Castle Cheeseburger	1 (2.3 oz)	200	—	11
White Castle Hamburger	1 (2.1 oz)	160	—	8
HERRING				
cooked	1 fillet (5 oz)	290	4	17
kippered	1 fillet (1.4 oz)	87	1	5
pickled	½ oz	39	tr	3
HOMINY				
Allen Golden	½ cup (4.5 oz)	120	0	1
Uncle William White	½ cup (4.5 oz)	100	0	1
HONEY				
Burleson's Clover	1 tbsp	60	0	0
Golden Blossom	1 tsp	20	0	0

FOOD	PORTION	CALS.	SAT. FAT	TOTAL FAT
HONEYDEW				
cubed	1 cup	60	—	tr
wedge	1/10	46	—	tr
HORSERADISH				
Gold's Hot	1 tsp	4	—	tr
Hebrew National White	1 tbsp	7	0	0
Rosoff's Red	1 tbsp (0.5 oz)	8	0	0
HOT DOG				
corndog	1	460	5	19
w/ bun chili	1	297	5	13
w/ bun plain	1	242	5	15
Armour Star Jumbo Beef	1	190	—	18
Empire Chicken	1 (2 oz)	100	2	7
Empire Turkey	1 (2 oz)	90	2	6
Health Valley Chicken Weiners	1	96	—	8
Healthy Choice	1 (1.6 oz)	60	1	2
Hebrew National Beef	1 (1.7 oz)	150	—	14
Hebrew National Cocktail Beef	6 (1.8 oz)	160	—	15
Hillshire Franks Jumbo Light & Mild	1 link	110	—	8
Hormel Big 8	1 (2 oz)	170	7	15
Hormel Light & Lean 97	1 (1.6 oz)	45	1	1
Louis Rich Turkey	1 (1.6 oz)	90	2	7
Oscar Mayer Big & Juicy Hot 'N Spicy	1 (2.7 oz)	220	8	20
Wampler Longacre Chicken	1 (2 oz)	130	—	11
HUMMUS				
hummus	1/3 cup	140	1	7
ICE CREAM AND FROZEN DESSERTS				
french vanilla soft serve	1 cup	377	14	23
gelato, chocolate hazelnut	1/2 cup (5.3 oz)	370	4	29
gelato, vanilla	1/2 cup (3 oz)	211	8	15
vanilla light soft serve	1 cup	223	3	5
Ben & Jerry's Cherry Garcia	1/2 cup (4 fl oz)	230	9	16
Ben & Jerry's Rain Forest Crunch	1/2 cup (4 fl oz)	270	10	21
Ben & Jerry's Vanilla	1/2 cup (4 fl oz)	215	9	16

FOOD	PORTION	CALS.	SAT. FAT	TOTAL FAT
Bon Bons Vanilla With Milk Chocolate Coating	8 pieces	330	13	23
Borden Fat Free Peach	½ cup	90	tr	tr
Borden Strawberry	½ cup	130	—	6
Breyers Butter Almond	½ cup	170	6	11
Breyers Cherry Vanilla	½ cup	150	5	7
Breyers French Vanilla	(2.5 oz)	170	6	10
Breyers Mint Chocolate Chip	½ cup (2.6 oz)	170	6	10
Breyers Reduced Fat Heavenly Hash	½ cup (2.4 oz)	150	3	5
Breyers Viennetta Vanilla	1 (4.2 fl oz)	160	8	10
DoveBar Chocolate Milk Chocolate	1 (3.8 fl oz)	340	13	21
Drumstick Cone Chocolate Dipped	1 (4.6 oz)	340	10	17
Edy's Light Almond Praline	4 oz	140	2–3	5
Edy's Light Butter Pecan	4 oz	140	2–3	5
Edy's Light Chocolate Chip	4 oz	120	2–3	4
Friendly's Heath English Toffee	½ cup (2.7 oz)	190	6	10
Frusen Gladje Chocolate	½ cup	240	9	17
Good Humor Ice Cream Sandwich	1	190	4	8
Good Humor King Cone	1 (5.7 fl oz)	300	11	14
Haagen-Dazs Coffee	4 oz	270	8	17
Haagen-Dazs Orange & Cream Pop	1	130	—	6
Haagen-Dazs Rum Raisin	4 oz	250	8	17
Haagen-Dazs Vanilla Fudge	4 oz	270	—	17
Healthy Choice Cookies 'N Cream	½ cup	120	2	2
Healthy Choice Rocky Road	½ cup (2.2 oz)	140	1	2
Healthy Choice Vanilla	½ cup (2.2 oz)	100	2	2
Light N' Lively Light Coffee	½ cup (2.4 oz)	110	2	3
Rice Dream Cappuccino	½ cup	130	—	5
Rice Dream Carob	½ cup	130	—	5
Rice Dream Lemon	½ cup	130	—	5
Sealtest Free Black Cherry	½ cup	100	0	0
Sealtest Free Chocolate	½ cup	100	0	0
Sealtest Free Strawberry	½ cup	100	0	0
Sealtest Free Vanilla	½ cup	100	0	0
Sealtest Maple Walnut	½ cup (2.4 oz)	160	5	9

FOOD	PORTION	CALS.	SAT. FAT	TOTAL FAT
Sealtest Vanilla Chocolate Strawberry	½ cup (2.4 oz)	140	4	6
Ultra Slim-Fast Vanilla	4 oz	90	—	tr
Ultra Slim-Fast Vanilla Chocolate Sandwich	1	140	—	2

ICE CREAM TOPPINGS

FOOD	PORTION	CALS.	SAT. FAT	TOTAL FAT
Hershey Chocolate Fudge	2 tbsp	100	—	4
Kraft Butterscotch	1 tbsp	60	0	1
Kraft Hot Fudge	1 tbsp	70	1	0
Kraft Strawberry	1 tbsp	50	0	0
Smucker's Carmel	2 tbsp	140	—	1
Smucker's Hot Fudge Light	2 tbsp	70	—	tr
Smucker's Marshmallow	2 tbsp	120	—	0
Smucker's Pecans In Syrup	2 tbsp	130	—	1
Smucker's Walnuts In Syrup	2 tbsp	130	—	1

ICED TEA

FOOD	PORTION	CALS.	SAT. FAT	TOTAL FAT
ice tea with lemon unsweetened	9 oz	4	0	0
Arizona Raspberry	8 fl oz	95	0	0
Clearly Tea Original Clearly Canadian	8 fl oz	80	—	0
Lipton Lemon	6 oz	55	—	0
Royal Mistic Lemon	12 fl oz	144	0	0

ICES AND ICE POPS

FOOD	PORTION	CALS.	SAT. FAT	TOTAL FAT
Ben & Jerry's Cherry Pop	1	330	—	24
Crystal Light Fruit Punch	1 bar	14	—	0
Cyrk Ice Chocolate	4 oz	85	tr	1
Dole Fruit 'n Juice Lemonade	1 bar (4 oz)	120	0	0
Fi-Bar Juice Bar Strawberry Nectar	1 bar	63	—	tr
Frozfruit Strawberry	1 (4 oz)	80	0	0
Frusen Gladje Sorbet Raspberry	½ cup	140	0	0
Good Humor Creamsicle Pop Orange	1 (1.8 fl oz)	70	1	2
Good Humor Fudgsicle Pop	1 (1.8 fl oz)	60	1	1
Good Humor Popsicle Rainbow Pops	1 (1.8 fl oz)	45	0	0
Good Humor Snow Cone	1	60	—	0

FOOD	PORTION	CALS.	SAT. FAT	TOTAL FAT
Haagen-Dazs Sorbet & Cream				
Orange	4 oz	190	—	8
Jell-O Mixed Berry	1 bar	31	—	tr
Kool-Aid Grape	1 bar	42	0	0
Lifesavers Ice Pops	1	35	0	0
Tofutti Frutti Apricot Mango Tofutti	4 fl oz	100	0	0
JAM/JELLY/PRESERVES				
BAMA Apple Butter	2 tsp	25	0	0
BAMA Apple Jelly	2 tsp	30	0	0
BAMA Grape Jelly	2 tsp	30	0	0
Kraft All Flavors Jam	1 tsp	17	0	0
Kraft All Flavors Jelly	1 tsp	17	0	0
Kraft All Flavors Preserves	1 tsp	17	0	0
Smucker's Low Sugar Spread All				
Flavors	1 tsp	8	0	0
Smucker's Orange Marmalade	1 tsp	18	0	0
Smucker's Simply Fruit All Flavors	1 tsp	16	0	0
Smucker's Simply Fruit Apple				
Butter	1 tsp	12	0	0
Weight Watchers Grape Spread	1 tsp	8	0	0
Whistling Wings Blueberry Jam	1 oz	50	—	tr
KALE				
chopped, cooked	½ cup	21	tr	tr
chopped, cooked frzn	½ cup	20	tr	tr
KEFIR				
kefir	3½ oz	66	—	4
KIDNEY BEANS				
canned	1 cup	208	tr	1
dried, cooked	1 cup	225	tr	1
KIWIS				
fresh	1 med	46	—	tr
KNISH				
potato	1 med (3.5 oz)	166	2	6
KOHLRABI				
raw, sliced	½ cup	19	tr	tr
sliced, cooked	½ cup	24	tr	tr

FOOD	PORTION	CALS.	SAT. FAT	TOTAL FAT
KUMQUATS				
fresh	1	12	—	tr
LAMB				
cubed lean only, broiled	3 oz	158	2	6
ground, broiled	3 oz	240	7	17
leg lean & fat Choice, roasted	3 oz	219	6	14
loin chop w/ bone lean & fat Choice, broiled	1 chop (2.3 oz)	201	6	15
rib chop lean & fat Choice, broiled	3 oz	307	11	25
shank lean & fat Choice, braised	3 oz	206	5	11
LAMB DISHES				
curry	¾ cup	345	3	17
moussaka	5.6 oz	312	—	21
stew	¾ cup	124	1	5
LEEKS				
chopped, cooked	¼ cup	8	tr	tr
LEMON				
fresh	1 med	22	tr	tr
wedge	1	5	tr	tr
LEMON JUICE				
bottled	1 tbsp	3	tr	tr
LEMONADE				
Bright & Early	8 fl oz	120	0	0
Country Time	8 fl oz	82	0	0
Crystal Geyser Juice Squeeze Pink	1 bottle (12 fl oz)	140	0	0
Crystal Light	8 fl oz	5	0	0
Diet Rite Salt/Sodium Free	8 fl oz	2	0	0
4C Instant, as prep	8 fl oz	80	—	0
Fruitopia	8 fl oz	120	0	0
Kool-Aid	8 fl oz	99	0	0
Kool-Aid Koolers Kool-Aid	1 pkg (8.45 fl oz)	120	0	0
Minute Maid Chilled	8 fl oz	110	0	0
Minute Maid frzn	8 fl oz	110	0	0
Mott's	10 fl oz	160	0	0
Nehi Royal Crown	8 fl oz	130	0	0
Newman's Own Roadside Virginia	8 fl oz	100	—	tr

FOOD	PORTION	CALS.	SAT. FAT	TOTAL FAT
Ocean Spray	8 fl oz	110	0	0
Royal Mistic Tropical Pink	16 fl oz	230	0	0
Seneca frzn	8 fl oz	110	0	0
Shasta	12 fl oz	146	—	0
Sipps	8.45 fl oz	85	—	0
Snapple	8 fl oz	110	0	0
Tropicana	8 fl oz	110	0	0
Veryfine	8 fl oz	120	0	0
Wylers	1 can (6 fl oz)	64	0	0
Wylers Drink Mix Unsweetened, as prep	8 fl oz	3	0	0
LENTILS				
dried, cooked	1 cup	231	tr	1
Health Valley Fast Menu Hearty Lentils Garden Vegetables	7½ oz	150	—	4
LETTUCE				
bibb	1 head (6 oz)	21	tr	tr
boston	2 leaves	2	tr	tr
looseleaf shredded	½ cup	5	tr	tr
romaine shredded	½ cup	4	tr	tr
Dole Butter	1 head	21	—	tr
Dole Iceberg	⅙ med head	20	—	0
LIMA BEANS				
dried baby, cooked	1 cup	229	tr	1
dried large, cooked	1 cup	217	tr	1
frzn, cooked	½ cup	94	tr	tr
large, canned	1 cup	191	tr	tr
LIME				
fresh	1	20	tr	tr
LIME JUICE				
Realime	1 oz	6	0	0
LIQUOR/LIQUEUR				
anisette	⅔ oz	74	—	0
apricot brandy	⅔ oz	64	—	0
benedictine	⅔ oz	69	—	0
bloody mary	5 oz	116	tr	tr

FOOD	PORTION	CALS.	SAT. FAT	TOTAL FAT
bourbon & soda	4 oz	105	0	0
coffee liqueur	1½ oz	174	tr	tr
coffee w/ cream liqueur	1½ oz	154	5	7
creme de menthe	1½ oz	186	tr	tr
curacao liqueur	⅔ oz	54	—	0
daiquiri	2 oz	111	0	0
gin & tonic	7.5 oz	171	0	0
manhattan	2 oz	128	0	0
martini	2½ oz	156	0	0
mint julep	10 oz	210	—	0
pina colada	4½ oz	262	1	3
planter's punch	3½ oz	175	—	0
rum	1½ oz	97	0	0
screwdriver	7 oz	174	tr	tr
tequila sunrise	5½ oz	189	tr	tr
vodka	1½ oz	97	0	0
whiskey sour	3 oz	123	tr	tr
LIVER				
beef, pan-fried	3 oz	184	2	7
chicken, stewed	1 cup (5 oz)	219	3	8
LOBSTER				
cooked	3 oz	83	tr	1
newburg	1 cup	485	—	27
Cajun Cookin' Crawfish Etouffee	12 oz	390	—	10
LOTUS				
root, raw sliced	10 slices	45	tr	tr
LUNCHEON MEATS/COLD CUTS				
blood sausage	1 oz	95	3	9
dried beef	5 slices (21 g)	35	—	tr
headcheese pork	1 oz	60	1	5
mortadella beef & pork	1 oz	88	3	7
pickle & pimiento loaf pork	1 oz	74	2	6
submarine w/ salami, ham, cheese, lettuce, tomato, onion & oil	1	456	7	19
Carl Buddig Corned Beef	1 oz	40	1	2

FOOD	PORTION	CALS.	SAT. FAT	TOTAL FAT
DiLusso Genoa	1 oz	100	4	8
Hebrew National Bologna Midget	2 oz	180	—	16
Hebrew National Deli Express Tongue Sliced	2 oz	120	—	9
Hillshire Brunschweiger	1 oz	95	—	8
Hillshire Pepperoni	1 oz	110	—	10
Hormel Liverwurst Spread	4 tbsp (2 oz)	130	4	10
Jones Liver Sausage	1 slice	80	—	7
Oscar Mayer Bologna Light	1 slice (1 oz)	60	2	4
Oscar Mayer Braunschweiger	2 oz	190	6	17
Oscar Mayer Cotto Salami	2 slices (1.6 oz)	100	4	8
Oscar Mayer Hard Salami	3 slices (1 oz)	100	3	9
Oscar Mayer Lunchables Bologna/ American	1 pkg (4.5 oz)	450	15	34
Oscar Mayer Lunchables Ham/ Swiss	1 pkg (4.5 oz)	320	8	17
Oscar Mayer Lunchables Pepperoni/American	1 pkg (4.5 oz)	480	17	36
Oscar Mayer Lunchables Salami/ American	1 pkg (4.5 oz)	430	15	32
Oscar Mayer Olive Loaf	1 slice (1 oz)	70	2	5
Russer Bologna	2 oz	180	7	15
Russer Pepper Loaf	2 oz	90	2	3
Spam	2 oz	170	6	16
Spam Lite	2 oz	110	3	8
Underwood Liverwurst	2.08 oz	180	—	15
Weight Watchers Bologna	2 slices (¾ oz)	35	—	2
LYCHEES				
fresh	1	6	—	tr
Ka-Me Whole Pitted In Syrup	15 pieces (5 oz)	130	0	0
MACADAMIA NUTS				
Mauna Loa Chocolate Covered	1 oz	170	—	13
Mauna Loa Roasted & Salted	1 oz	210	—	21
MACKEREL				
cooked	3 oz	134	2	5

FOOD	PORTION	CALS.	SAT. FAT	TOTAL FAT
cooked	1 fillet (5.1 oz)	230	3	9
Empress	4 oz	140	—	8
MALT				
nonalcoholic	12 fl oz	32	0	0
Bartles & Jaymes Malt Cooler				
Original	12 fl oz	180	0	0
Olde English	12 oz	163	0	0
Schaefer	12 oz	165	0	0
Schlitz	12 oz	177	0	0
MALTED MILK				
chocolate, as prep w/ milk	1 cup	229	6	9
MANGO				
fresh	1	135	tr	1
MANGO JUICE				
Kern's Nectar	6 fl oz	100	0	0
MARGARINE				
diet	1 tsp	17	tr	2
squeeze	1 tsp	34	1	4
stick	1 tsp	39	1	4
stick, unsalted	1 tsp	34	1	4
tub	1 tsp	34	1	4
tub, unsalted	1 tsp	34	1	4
MARSHMALLOW				
Campfire	2 lg	40	0	0
Funmallows Miniature	10	18	0	0
Marshmallow Fluff	1 heaping tsp (18 g)	59	—	tr
MATZO				
Manischewitz Egg Milk Chocolate Coated Horowitz Margareten	1 oz	97	3	4
Manischewitz Matzo Cracker Miniatures	10	90	—	tr
Manischewitz Passover	1	129	—	tr
Manischewitz Unsalted	1	110	0	tr
Streit's Whole Wheat	1 (1 oz)	110	0	1
MAYONNAISE				
mayonnaise	1 tbsp	99	2	11

FOOD	PORTION	CALS.	SAT. FAT	TOTAL FAT
Best Foods Cholesterol Free Reduced Calorie	1 tbsp (15 g)	50	1	5
Best Foods Real	1 tbsp	100	2	11
Hain Light Low Sodium	1 tbsp	60	1	6
Hellmann's	1 tbsp	100	2	11
Hellmann's Light Reduced Calorie	1 tbsp (15 g)	50	1	5
Hellmann's Cholesterol Free Reduced Calorie	1 tbsp (15 g)	50	1	5
Kraft Free	1 tbsp	12	0	0
Kraft Light	1 tbsp	50	1	5
Kraft Real	1 tbsp	100	2	12
Kraft Sandwich Spread	1 tbsp	50	1	5
Smart Beat Canola Oil	1 tbsp	40	tr	4
Weight Watchers Fat Free	1 tbsp	12	0	0
Weight Watchers Light	1 tbsp	50	1	5
MAYONNAISE TYPE SALAD DRESSING				
Miracle Whip	1 tbsp	70	1	7
Miracle Whip Free	1 tbsp	20	0	0
Miracle Whip Light	1 tbsp	45	1	4
Spin Blend	1 tbsp	60	1	5
MEAT STICKS				
Tomstone Beef Jerky	1	35	0	0
Tombstone Beef Sticks	1	110	5	10
MEAT SUBSTITUTES				
Ken & Robert's Veggie Burger	1 (62 g)	110	0	2
LaLoma Big Franks	1 (51 g)	110	—	6
LaLoma Vege-Burger	½ cup (108 g)	110	—	2
Lightlife Smart Dogs	1 (1.5 oz)	40	0	0
Lightlife Tofu Pups	1 (1.5 oz)	92	—	5
Morningstar Farms Deli Franks	1 (35 g)	90	—	6
Sovex Better Than Burger	½ cup (1.9 oz)	165	1	2
White Wave Meatless Healthy Franks	1 (1.5 oz)	90	0	2
White Wave Meatless Sandwich Slices Bologna	2 slices (1.6 oz)	120	2	8

FOOD	PORTION	CALS.	SAT. FAT	TOTAL FAT
White Wave Veggie Burger	1 patty (2.5 oz)	110	0	3
Worthington Vegetarian Burger	½ cup (113 g)	150	—	4
MELON				
Big Valley Mixed frzn	¾ cup (4.9 oz)	40	0	0
MILK				
buttermilk	1 cup	99	1	2
skim	1 cup	86	tr	tr
whole	1 cup	150	5	8
1%	1 cup	102	2	3
2%	1 cup	121	3	5
Borden Acidophilus 1%	8 fl oz	100	—	2
CalciMilk	8 fl oz	102	2	3
Carnation Evaporated	2 tbsp	40	2	3
Carnation Evaporated Lowfat	2 tbsp	25	—	1
Carnation Sweetened Condensed	2 tbsp	130	2	3
Carnation Lite Evaporated Skimmed Carnation	½ cup (4 fl oz)	100	—	tr
Farmland Cholesterol Reduced	8 oz	150	—	8
Lactaid 1%	8 fl oz	102	2	3
MILK DRINKS				
Bosco Chocolate Milk	1 cup (8 fl oz)	230	—	8
Hershey Whole Chocolate Milk	8 fl oz	210	—	9
Quik Chocolate Lowfat Milk	8 fl oz	200	—	5
Quik Ready To Drink Strawberry	8 fl oz	230	—	8
MILK SUBSTITUTES				
Better Than Milk Carob	8 fl oz	130	—	5
Better Than Milk Chocolate	8 fl oz	125	—	5
Edensoy	8.45 fl oz	140	1	4
First Alternative	8 fl oz	80	tr	2
Healthy Valley Soo Moo Health Valley	1 cup	120	—	6
Rice Dream Organic Original Lite	8 fl oz	130	—	2
Spring Creek Original	1 oz	21	—	5
Vegelicious	8 fl oz	100	—	2
Westsoy Plain Lite	8 fl oz	100	tr	2

FOOD	PORTION	CALS.	SAT. FAT	TOTAL FAT
MILKSHAKE				
chocolate	10 oz	360	7	11
strawberry	10 oz	319	—	8
vanilla	10 oz	314	5	8
MINERAL/BOTTLED WATER				
Canada Dry Sparkling Water	8 fl oz	0	0	0
Crystal Geyser Sparkling Lemon	1 bottle (12 fl oz)	0	0	0
Evian	1 liter	0	0	0
LaCroix Sparkling Berry	12 fl oz	0	0	0
San Pellegrino	1 liter (33.8 oz)	0	0	0
Saratoga Sparkling	1 liter	0	0	0
MISO				
miso	½ cup	284	1	8
MONKFISH				
baked	3 oz	82	—	2
MOUSSE				
Weight Watchers Chocolate	1 (2.5 oz)	160	tr	3
MUFFIN				
blueberry	1 (2 oz)	158	1	4
corn	1 (2 oz)	174	1	5
toaster type, corn	1	114	1	4
toaster type, wheat bran w/ raisins	1 (36 g)	106	1	3
Health Valley Fat Free Apple Spice	1	140	—	tr
Hostess Mini Chocolate Chip	5 (2 oz)	260	5	15
Hostess Oat Bran	1 (1.5 oz)	160	1	8
Pepperidge Farm Blueberry	1	170	1	7
Pepperidge Farm Corn	1	180	1	7
Sara Lee Apple Spice	1	220	—	8
Sara Lee Oat Bran	1	210	—	8
Sara Lee Raisin Bran	1	220	—	7
Weight Watchers Lemon Poppy Seed	1 (2.5 oz)	200	2	5
MUNG BEANS				
sprouts canned	½ cup	8	tr	tr
sprouts stir fried	½ cup	31	tr	tr

FOOD	PORTION	CALS.	SAT. FAT	TOTAL FAT
MUSHROOMS				
chanterelle canned	3½ oz	12	—	1
chanterelle fresh	3½ oz	11	—	tr
enoki raw	1 (4 in)	2	tr	tr
morel fresh	3½ oz	9	—	tr
oyster fresh	3.5 oz	11	—	tr
shiitake, cooked	4 (2.5 oz)	40	tr	tr
Empress Button	2 oz	14	0	0
Green Giant Oriental Straw	¼ cup	12	0	0
MUSSELS				
cooked	3 oz	147	1	4
MUSTARD				
Grey Poupon Dijon	1 tsp	6	0	0
Heinz Spicy Brown	1 tbsp	14	—	1
Kraft Horseradish Mustard	1 tbsp	14	0	1
Plochman Stone Ground	1 tsp (5 g)	6	—	tr
Russer Deli	1 tsp (5 g)	4	0	0
MUSTARD GREENS				
chopped, cooked	½ cup	11	tr	tr
chopped, cooked frzn	½ cup	14	tr	tr
NAVY BEANS				
canned	1 cup	296	tr	1
dried, cooked	1 cup	259	tr	1
NECTARINE				
fresh	1	67	—	1
NEUFCHATEL				
neufchatel	1 oz	74	4	7
Philadelphia Brand Light	1 oz	80	4	7
Spreadery With Strawberries	1 oz	70	3	5
NOODLES				
cellophane	1 cup	492	tr	tr
egg, cooked	1 cup	212	tr	2
japanese soba, cooked	½ cup	56	tr	tr
noodle pudding	½ cup	132	4	7
Azumaya Chinese	4 oz	293	—	1
La Choy Chow Mein Narrow	½ cup	150	1	8

FOOD	PORTION	CALS.	SAT. FAT	TOTAL FAT
La Choy Rice	½ cup	130	—	5
Shofar No Yolks	2 oz	210	0	0
NUTRITIONAL SUPPLEMENTS				
Fi-Bar Apple	1 bar (1 oz)	90	—	3
Figurines Chocolate	1 bar	100	—	5
Meal On The Go Original	1 bar (3 oz)	286	2	9
Nestle Sweet Success Bar Chewy Chocolate Chip	1 bar (1.6 oz)	120	2	4
Sego Lite Chocolate	10 fl oz	150	—	3
Slim-Fast Nutrition Bar Peanut Butter	1 bar	140	—	6
Slim-Fast Powder Strawberry, as prep w/ skim milk	8 fl oz	190	—	1
Ultra Slim-Fast Cafe Mocha, as prep w/ skim milk	8 fl oz	200	—	tr
Ultra Slim-Fast Crunch Bar Vanilla Almond	1 bar	110	—	4
Ultra Slim-Fast French Vanilla, as prep w/ skim milk	8 fl oz	190	—	tr
Ultra Slim-Fast Fruit Juice Mix, as prep w/ fruit juice	8 fl oz	200	—	tr
Ultra Slim-Fast Ready-to-Drink Chocolate Royale	12 fl oz	250	—	1
Vita-J Fruit Punch	1 bottle (11.5 fl oz)	8	0	0
NUTS MIXED				
dry roasted w/ peanuts, salted	1 oz	169	2	15
oil roasted w/ peanuts, salted	1 oz	175	2	16
OCTOPUS				
fresh steamed	3 oz	140	tr	2
OIL				
canola	1 tbsp	124	2	14
corn	1 tbsp	120	2	14
cottonseed	1 tbsp	120	4	14
hazelnut	1 tbsp	120	1	14
olive	1 tbsp	119	2	14
peanut	1 tbsp	119	2	14

FOOD	PORTION	CALS.	SAT. FAT	TOTAL FAT
safflower	1 tbsp	120	1	14
soybean	1 tbsp	120	2	14
sunflower	1 tbsp	120	1	14
walnut	1 tbsp	120	1	14
wheat germ	1 tbsp	120	3	14
Hain Cod Liver	1 tbsp	120	—	14
House of Tsang Hot Chili Sesame	1 tsp (5 g)	45	1	5
House of Tsang Mongolian Fire	1 tsp (5 g)	45	1	5
Mazola No Stick	2.5 sec spray (0.2 g)	2	tr	tr
Pam	1 sec spray (0.266 g)	2	—	tr
Weight Watchers Butter Spray	1 sec spray	2	0	tr
Wesson Cooking Spray Lite	0.5 sec spray	0	—	0
OKRA				
sliced, cooked	½ cup	25	tr	tr
sliced, cooked	8 pods	27	tr	tr
Hanover Whole	½ cup	35	—	0
Trappey's Cocktail Hot	2 pieces (1 oz)	8	tr	tr
OLIVES				
green	4 med	15	tr	2
green	3 extra lg	15	tr	2
ripe	1 sm	4	tr	tr
ripe	1 lg	5	tr	tr
Progresso Olive Appetizer	½ cup	180	3	21
ONION				
fried	½ cup (7.5 oz)	176	6	11
raw, chopped	1 tbsp	4	tr	tr
scallions raw, chopped	1 tbsp	2	tr	tr
Antioch Farms Vidalia	1 med	60	—	0
Birds Eye Small With Cream Sauce	½ cup	100	1	3
Ore Ida Onion Ringers	6 pieces (3 oz)	240	3	14
S&W Whole Small	½ cup	35	0	0
ORANGE				
california navel	1	65	tr	tr
california valencia	1	59	tr	tr
florida	1	69	tr	tr

FOOD	PORTION	CALS.	SAT. FAT	TOTAL FAT
sections	1 cup	85	tr	tr
S&W Mandarin Natural Style	½ cup	60	0	0
ORANGE JUICE				
frzn, as prep	1 cup	112	tr	tr
orange drink	6 oz	94	0	0
Bright & Early Chilled	8 fl oz	120	0	0
Hi-C	8 fl oz	130	0	0
Minute Maid Box	8.45 fl oz	120	0	0
Sippin' Pak 100% Pure	8.45 fl oz	110	0	0
Tang Breakfast Crystals, as prep	6 oz	86	0	0
Tropicana	1 container (6 fl oz)	80	0	0
Tropicana Season's Best	8 fl oz	110	0	0
ORIENTAL FOOD				
chicken teriyaki	¾ cup	399	6	27
chop suey w/ pork	1 cup	375	8	29
chow mein shrimp	1 cup	221	1	10
fried rice	6.6 oz	249	—	6
wonton soup	1 cup	205	1	3
wonton fried	½ cup (1 oz)	111	1	8
Birds Eye Chicken Teriyaki Easy Recipe, not prep	½ pkg	160	1	4
Chun King Beef Pepper Oriental	13 oz	319	—	3
Chun King Egg Rolls Chicken	1 (3.6 oz)	220	—	8
Chun King Sweet & Sour Pork	13 oz	400	—	5
La Choy Bi-Pack Chow Mein Chicken	¾ cup	80	1	3
La Choy Entree Beef Pepper Oriental	¾ cup	100	2	4
Tyson Sweet & Sour Kit With Sweet & Sour Sauce	14.85 oz	440	—	9
Worthington Vegetarian Egg Rolls	1 (85 g)	160	—	6
OYSTERS				
battered & fried	6 (4.9 oz)	368	5	18
fresh raw	6 med	58	1	2
oysters rockefeller	3 oysters	66	—	2
steamed	1 med	41	tr	1

FOOD	PORTION	CALS.	SAT. FAT	TOTAL FAT
stew	1 cup	278	10	18
Bumble Bee Whole	½ cup (3.5 oz)	100	1	4
PANCAKE/WAFFLE SYRUP				
low calorie	1 tbsp	12	0	0
maple	2 tbsp	122	0	0
PANCAKES				
buckwheat	1 (4 in diam)	55	1	2
potato	1 (4 in diam)	78	1	6
w/ butter & syrup	3	519	6	14
whole wheat	1 (4 in diam)	92	1	3
Aunt Jemima Blueberry	3.48 oz	220	1	4
Aunt Jemima Original	3.48 oz	211	—	4
Downyflake Buttermilk	3	280	—	9
PAPAYA				
cubed	1 cup	54	tr	tr
PAPAYA JUICE				
Goya Nectar	6 oz	110	—	0
PARSLEY				
dried	1 tbsp	1	tr	tr
fresh chopped	1 tbsp	4	tr	tr
PARSNIPS				
cooked, sliced	½ cup	63	tr	tr
PASTA				
elbows, cooked	1 cup	197	tr	tr
shells, cooked	1 cup	197	tr	tr
spaghetti, cooked	1 cup	197	tr	tr
whole wheat spaghetti, cooked	1 cup	174	tr	tr
San Giorgio Ziti	2 oz	210	—	1
PASTA DINNERS				
rigatoni w/ sausage sauce	¾ cup	260	4	12
Banquet Lasagne w/ Meat Sauce	7 oz	270	—	10
Budget Gourmet Cheese Manicotti	1 pkg (10 oz)	440	—	24
Budget Gourmet Vegetable Lasagna	1 pkg (10.5 oz)	390	5	10
Chef Boyardee ABC's & 1,2,3's In Cheese Flavor Sauce	7.5 oz	180	tr	1

FOOD	PORTION	CALS.	SAT. FAT	TOTAL FAT
Chef Boyardee Beef Ravioli	7.5 oz	190	2	4
Chef Boyardee Beefaroni	7.5 oz	220	1	7
Chef Boyardee Microwave Main Meal Lasagna	10.5 oz	290	—	8
Chef Boyardee Rings & Franks	7.5 oz	190	2	5
Dining Light Fettucini	9 oz	290	—	12
Dinty Moore Noodles & Chicken	1 can (7.5 oz)	180	2	8
Formagg Penne Pasta Primavera	⅔ cup (5 oz)	190	0	2
Franco-American Macaroni & Cheese	½ can (7⅜ oz)	170	—	6
Franco-American SpaghettiO's With Meatballs	½ can (7⅜ oz)	220	—	9
Golden Grain Macaroni & Cheese	½ cup	310	—	15
Green Giant One Serve Cheese Tortellini	1 pkg	260	3	9
Healthy Choice Classics Pasta Shells Marinara	1 meal (12 oz)	360	2	3
Healthy Choice Macaroni & Cheese	1 meal (9 oz)	290	2	5
Healthy Choice Spaghetti Bolognese	1 meal (10 oz)	260	1	3
Hormel Micro Cup Meals Macaroni And Cheese	1 cup (7.5 oz)	260	6	11
Kraft Deluxe Dinner Macaroni & Cheese	¾ cup	260	4	8
Lean Cuisine Macaroni And Beef	1 pkg (10 oz)	280	2	8
Lean Cuisine Tuna Lasagna	1 pkg (9.75 oz)	230	2	6
Le Menu Entree LightStyle, Spaghetti With Beef Sauce And Mushrooms	9 oz	280	—	6
Lipton Pasta And Sauce Cheddar Broccoli	½ cup	132	—	2
Morton Spaghetti & Meat Sauce	8.5 oz	170	—	2
Mrs. Paul's Seafood Rotini	9 oz	240	2	6
Palmazone Macaroni 'n Cheese	½ pkg (6 oz)	260	—	7
Stouffer's Cheese Manocotti	1 pkg (9 oz)	340	7	16
Stouffer's Lunch Express Chicken Fettucini	1 pkg (10.25 oz)	250	3	6

FOOD	PORTION	CALS.	SAT. FAT	TOTAL FAT
Stouffer's Turkey Tettrazini	1 pkg (10 oz)	360	3	19
Ultra Slim-Fast Macaroni & Cheese	2.3 oz	230	—	3
Ultra Slim-Fast Pasta Primavera	12 oz	340	—	9
Uncle Ben Country Inn Pasta And Sauce Angel Hair Parmesan	1 serv (2.2 oz)	245	—	5
Velvetta Dinner Bits of Bacon And Cheese	½ cup	240	5	10
Weight Watchers Fettucini Alfredo	8 oz	230	2	7
PASTA FRESH				
spinach made w/ egg, cooked	2 oz	74	tr	tr
Contadina Angel's Hair	1¼ cup (2.8 oz)	240	1	3
Contadina Fettuccine	1¼ cup (2.9 oz)	250	1	4
Contadina Ravioli Cheese	1 cup (3.1 oz)	280	6	12
Contadina Tortelloni Chicken And Prosciutto	1 cup (3.8 oz)	360	4	13
PASTA SALAD				
elbow macaroni salad	3.5 oz	160	2	5
italian style pasta salad	3.5 oz	140	1	7
pasta salad w/ vegetables	3.5 oz	140	3	4
PATE				
Sells Liver	2.08 oz	190	—	16
PEACH				
dried halves	10	311	tr	1
fresh	1	37	tr	tr
halves juice pack	1 half	34	tr	tr
Libby Yellow Cling Halves Lite	½ cup (4.4 oz)	60	0	0
S&W Freestone Halves Diet	½ cup	30	0	0
S&W Yellow Cling Sliced Premium In Heavy Syrup	½ cup	100	0	0
PEACH JUICE				
Goya Nectar	6 oz	110	—	0
PEANUT BUTTER				
Arrowhead Creamy	2 tbsp (1.1 oz)	200	3	15
BAMA Crunchy	2 tbsp	200	—	17
Health Valley Chunky No Salt	2 tbsp	170	—	14
Jif Creamy	2 tbsp (1.1 oz)	190	3	16

FOOD	PORTION	CALS.	SAT. FAT	TOTAL FAT
Peter Pan Creamy	2 tbsp	190	2	16
Reese's Peanut Butter Flavored Chips	¼ cup (1.5 oz)	230	—	13
Simply Jif Creamy	2 tbsp (1.1 oz)	180	3	16
Skippy Creamy, w/ 2 slices white bread	1 sandwich	340	3	19
Skippy Reduced Fat Creamy	2 tbsp	190	3	12
Smucker's Goober Grape	2 tbsp	180	2	10
Smucker's Natural	2 tbsp	200	3	16
PEANUTS				
oil roasted w/o salt	1 oz	163	2	14
spanish oil roasted w/o salt	1 oz	162	2	14
Eagle Honey Roasted	1 oz	170	—	13
PEAR				
asian	1 (4.3 oz)	51	tr	tr
dried halves	10	459	tr	1
pear	1	98	tr	1
Hunt's Halves	4 oz	90	—	tr
Libby Lite Halves canned	½ cup (4.3 oz)	60	0	0
PEAR JUICE				
Libby Nectar	1 can (11.5 fl oz)	220	0	0
PEAS				
dried split, cooked	1 cup	231	tr	1
edible-pod, cooked	½ cup	34	tr	tr
edible-pod, raw	½ cup	30	tr	tr
pea curry	1 serv (4.4 oz)	438	—	42
Birds Eye In Butter Sauce	½ cup	80	1	2
Crest Top Early June	½ cup (4.5 oz)	100	0	1
Green Giant Harvest Fresh Sugar Snap	½ cup	30	0	0
Green Giant Le Seur Early Select	½ cup	60	0	0
La Choy Snow Pea Pods	½ pkg (3 oz)	35	—	tr
S&W Petit Pois	½ cup	70	0	0
PECANS				
dry roasted	1 oz	187	1	18

FOOD	PORTION	CALS.	SAT. FAT	TOTAL FAT
PECTIN				
Sure-Jell	¼ pkg	38	—	0
PEPPERS				
chili green hot raw	1	18	tr	tr
green raw	1 (2.6 oz)	20	tr	tr
red raw	1 (2.6 oz)	20	tr	tr
yellow raw	10 strips	14	—	tr
Chi-Chi's Chilies Diced Green	2 tbsp (1.2 oz)	10	0	0
Progresso Piccalilli	½ cup	190	3	20
Progresso Roasted	½ cup	20	tr	tr
Trappey's Jalapeno Hot Sliced	21 slices (1 oz)	4	tr	tr
Trappey's Jalapeno Whole	2 peppers (1 oz)	11	tr	0
PERCH				
cooked	3 oz	99	tr	1
Van De Kamp's Battered	2 pieces	310	4	21
PERSIMMONS				
fresh	1	32	—	tr
fresh japanese	1	118	—	tr
PICKLES				
gherkins	3½ oz	21	—	tr
sweet	1 (1.2 oz)	41	tr	tr
Claussen Dill Spears	1 spear	4	—	tr
Hebrew National Half Sour	½ pickle (1 oz)	4	0	0
Vlasic Bread & Butter Chips	1 oz	30	0	0
Vlasic Kosher Baby Dills	1 oz	4	0	0
PIE				
apple fried	1 (6.4 oz)	404	3	21
blueberry	1 slice (4.4 oz)	289	2	13
blueberry fried	1 (6.4 oz)	404	3	21
cherry fried	1 (6.4 oz)	404	3	21
chocolate creme	1 slice (4 oz)	344	6	22
lemon fried	1 (6.4 oz)	404	3	21
lemon meringue	1 slice (4.5 oz)	303	2	10
peach	4 oz	261	2	12
peach fried	1 (6.4 oz)	404	3	21
strawberry fried	1 (6.4 oz)	404	3	21

FOOD	PORTION	CALS.	SAT. FAT	TOTAL FAT
Banquet Apple	1 slice (3.3 oz)	250	—	11
Banquet Pumpkin	1 slice (3.3 oz)	200	—	8
Drake's Apple	1 (2 oz)	210	—	10
Drake's Cherry	1 (2 oz)	220	—	10
Drake's Lemon	1 (2 oz)	210	—	11
Lance Pecan	1 (38 g)	350	3	15
Little Debbie Marshmallow Banana	1 pkg (1.4 oz)	160	3	5
Little Debbie Marshmallow Chocolate	1 pkg (1.4 oz)	160	3	5
Little Debbie Raisin Creme	1 pkg (1.2 oz)	140	1	5
McMillin's Lemon	4 oz	450	—	25
Mrs. Smith's Banana Cream	¼ of 8 in pie (3.4 oz)	250	3	9
Mrs. Smith's Boston Cream	⅛ of 8 in pie (2.4 oz)	170	2	5
Mrs. Smith's Cherry	⅒ of 10 in pie (4.6 oz)	410	—	18
Mrs. Smith's Mince	⅙ of 8 in pie (4.3 oz)	300	2	11
Mrs. Smith's Strawberry Rhubarb	⅕ of 8 in pie (4.8 oz)	520	4	23
Pepperidge Farm Mississippi Mud	1	310	12	23
Pet-Ritz Coconut Cream	⅙ pie (2.33 oz)	190	—	8
Pet-Ritz Sweet Potato	⅙ pie (3.33 oz)	150	—	7
Sara Lee Pecan Homestyle	1 slice (3.4 oz)	400	—	18
Tastykake Banana Creme	1 pkg (120 g)	380	6	16
Tastykake Blueberry	1 pkg (113 g)	310	2	9
Tastykake Peach	1 pkg (113 g)	300	3	12
Tastykake Pineapple Cheese	1 pkg (120 g)	340	3	13
Tastykake Pumpkin	1 pkg (4 oz)	320	4	14
Tastykake Strawberry	1 pkg (113 g)	340	3	11

PIEROGI

FOOD	PORTION	CALS.	SAT. FAT	TOTAL FAT
Mrs. T's Potato and Cheddar Cheese	1 (1.3 oz)	60	—	tr
Mrs. T's Potato And Onion	1 (1.3 oz)	50	—	tr
Mrs. T's Sauerkraut	1	60	—	0

FOOD	PORTION	CALS.	SAT. FAT	TOTAL FAT
PIGEON PEAS				
dried, cooked	½ cup	102	tr	tr
PIKE				
baked	3 oz	101	tr	1
PIMIENTOS				
Dromedary	1 oz	10	0	0
PINE NUTS				
pignolia dried	1 tbsp	51	1	5
PINEAPPLE				
fresh, diced	1 cup	77	tr	tr
fresh, sliced	1 slice	42	tr	tr
slices water pack	1 slice	19	tr	tr
Dole All Cuts Juice Pack	½ cup	70	—	tr
Dole All Cuts Syrup Pack	½ cup	90	0	0
PINEAPPLE JUICE				
Dole 100% frzn, as prep	8 fl oz	130	0	0
Minute Maid Box	8.45 fl oz	130	0	0
PINK BEANS				
dried, cooked	1 cup	252	tr	1
Goya Spanish Style	7.5 oz	140	—	tr
PINTO BEANS				
canned	1 cup	186	tr	1
dried, cooked	1 cup	235	tr	1
PISTACHIOS				
dry roasted, salted	1 oz	172	2	15
PIZZA				
cheese	⅛ of 12 in pie	184	2	5
cheese, meat & vegetables	⅛ of 12 in pie	184	2	5
Empire Bagel	1 (2 oz)	150	3	5
Fox Deluxe Golden Topping	½ pizza	240	—	11
Healthy Choice French Bread Pepperoni	1 (6 oz)	360	4	9
Jeno's 4-Pack Hamburger	1 pizza	180	—	9
Lean Cuisine French Bread Deluxe	1 pkg (6.1 oz)	350	3	6
Mr. P's Combination	½ pizza	260	—	13

FOOD	PORTION	CALS.	SAT. FAT	TOTAL FAT
Pappalo's French Bread Sausage	1 pizza	410	—	18
Pillsbury Microwave Cheese	½ pizza	240	—	10
Stouffer's French Bread Cheese	1 piece (5.2 oz)	350	5	14
Tombstone 12 in Light Vegetable	⅕ pie (4.6 oz)	240	3	7
Tombstone Double Top Double Cheese	⅙ pie (4.6 oz)	350	10	19
Tombstone For One ½ Less Fat Cheese	1 pie (6.5 oz)	360	5	10
Totino's Party Bacon	½ pizza	370	—	20
Weight Watchers Sausage	1 (6.43 oz)	340	2	10
PLANTAINS				
ripe, fried	2.8 oz	214	—	7
sliced, cooked	½ cup	89	—	tr
Top Banana All Natural Plantain Chips	1 oz	150	—	8
PLUMS				
fresh	1	36	tr	tr
purple in heavy syrup	3	119	tr	tr
purple in light syrup	1 cup	158	tr	tr
POI				
poi	½ cup	134	tr	tr
POLENTA				
Aurora	½ cup (5 oz)	110	0	0
POLLACK				
baked	5.3 oz	178	tr	2
POMEGRANATES				
pomegranates	1	104	—	tr
POMPANO				
florida, cooked	3 oz	179	4	10
POPCORN				
air-popped	1 cup	30	tr	tr
popped w/ vegetable oil	1 cup	55	1	3
Barrel O' Fun	1 oz	160	1	12
Cape Cod Light	½ oz	60	—	3
Chesters Cheddar Cheese	0.5 oz	80	—	5
Cracker Jack	1 oz	120	—	3

FOOD	PORTION	CALS.	SAT. FAT	TOTAL FAT
Jiffy Pop Bag Butter	3 cups	90	1	5
Lance Cheese	1 pkg (25 g)	130	1	8
Louise's Low-Fat Buttered	2½ cups (1 oz)	130	1	3
Newman's Own Oldstyle Picture Show	3⅓ cups	80	—	1
Orville Redenbacher's Gourmet Hot Air	3 cups	40	—	tr
Pillsbury Microwave Butter	3 cups	210	—	13
Pop Secret Butter Flavor	3 cups	100	tr	6
Pop Secret Light Butter Flavor	3 cups	70	1	3
Pop Secret Pop Chips	1½ cups (1 oz)	130	1	4
Smartfood Cheddar Cheese	0.5 oz	80	—	5
Snyder's Butter	1 oz	140	—	9
Ultra Slim-Fast Lite N' Tasty	½ oz	60	—	2
Weight Watchers Microwave	1 oz	100	—	1
PORK				
center loin chop, broiled	1 (3.1 oz)	275	7	24
center loin, roasted	3 oz	259	7	18
ham fresh rump half lean & fat, roasted	3 oz	233	—	23
rib chop lean only, broiled	1 chop (2.1 oz)	162	—	9
rib chop lean & fat, panfried	1 chop (2.9 oz)	343	—	29
spareribs, braised	3 oz	338	10	26
tenderloin lean only, roasted	3 oz	141	1	4
POT PIE				
Empire Chicken	1 (8.1 oz)	440	5	21
Morton Beef	7 oz	430	—	31
Stouffer's Turkey	1 cup (8 oz)	500	8	31
POTATO				
au gratin w/ cheese	½ cup	178	4	10
baked topped w/ cheese sauce	1	475	11	29
baked topped w/ sour cream & chives	1	394	10	22
baked w/ skin	1 (6½ oz)	220	tr	tr
boiled	½ cup	68	tr	tr
french fries	1 reg serv	235	4	12

FOOD	PORTION	CALS.	SAT. FAT	TOTAL FAT
french fries	10 strips	111	2	4
french fries thick cut	10 strips	109	2	4
hash brown	½ cup	151	4	9
hashed brown	½ cup	170	4	9
mashed w/ whole milk & margarine	⅓ cup	66	tr	tr
microwaved	1 (7 oz)	212	tr	tr
potato puffs	½ cup	138	3	7
potato salad	½ cup	179	2	10
scalloped	½ cup	127	—	5
Butterfield Whole	2½ pieces (5.6 oz)	90	0	0
Hormel Micro Cup Meals Scalloped Potatoes & Ham	1 cup (10.4 oz)	360	7	23
Yukon Gold	1 (5.3 oz)	110	—	0
PRETZELS				
A & Eagle	1 oz	110	—	2
Barrel O' Fun Mini	1 oz	110	0	1
J&J Soft	1 (2.25 oz)	170	—	0
Lance Twist	1 pkg (42 g)	150	0	1
Mister Salty Dutch	1 oz	110	tr	1
Mr. Phipps Chips	8 (0.5 oz)	60	tr	1
Quinlan Logs	1 oz	110	1	2
Rold Gold Rods	3 pieces (1 oz)	110	—	2
Snyder's Stix	1 oz	310	0	0
Ultra Slim-Fast Lite N' Tasty	1 oz	100	—	tr
Wege Sourdough	1 oz	102	—	tr
Wege Whole Wheat	1 oz	109	—	1
PRUNE JUICE				
canned	1 cup	181	tr	tr
PRUNES				
dried	10	201	tr	tr
in heavy syrup	5	90	tr	tr
Sunsweet Orange Essence Pitted Prunes	6 (1.4 oz)	100	0	0
PUDDING				
bread w/ raisins	½ cup	180	2	5

FOOD	PORTION	CALS.	SAT. FAT	TOTAL FAT
rice pudding	1 serv (3 oz)	110	—	4
rice w/ raisins	½ cup	246	3	6
Jell-O Chocolate	1 (4 oz)	171	—	6
Jell-O Chocolate Vanilla Swirl	1 (5.5 oz)	240	—	8
Jell-O Light Chocolate Fudge	1 (4 oz)	101	—	1
Jell-O Light Vanilla	1 (4 oz)	104	—	2
Jell-O Vanilla	1 (5.5 oz)	250	—	9
Snack Pack Banana	4.25 oz	145	1	6
Snack Pack Butterscotch	4.25 oz	170	1	6
Snack Pack Lemon	4.25 oz	150	1	4
Swiss Miss Tapioca	4 oz	160	1	5
PUDDING POPS				
Jell-O Chocolate	1 pop	79	—	2
Jell-O Vanilla	1 pop	77	—	2
PUMPKIN				
canned	½ cup	41	tr	tr
fresh cooked, mashed	½ cup	24	tr	tr
seeds, salted & roasted	1 oz	148	2	12
PURSLANE				
cooked	1 cup	21	—	tr
QUICHE				
cheese	1 slice (3 oz)	283	—	20
lorraine	1 slice (3 oz)	352	—	25
mushroom	1 slice (3 oz)	256	—	18
QUINOA				
quinoa	½ cup	318	tr	5
RADICCHIO				
raw shredded	½ cup	5	—	tr
RADISHES				
daikon raw, sliced	½ cup	8	tr	tr
raw	10	7	tr	tr
white icicle raw, sliced	½ cup	7	tr	tr
RAISINS				
golden seedless	1 cup	437	tr	1
seedless	1 tbsp	27	tr	tr

FOOD	PORTION	CALS.	SAT. FAT	TOTAL FAT
RASPBERRIES				
fresh	1 cup	61	tr	1
Big Valley frzn	⅔ cup (4.9 oz)	80	0	0
RASPBERRY JUICE				
Smucker's Juice Sparkler	10 oz	130	—	tr
RED BEANS				
red beans, cooked	½ cup	90	—	0
Van Camp's	½ cup (4.6 oz)	90	0	0
RELISH				
cranberry orange	½ cup	246	—	tr
hamburger	1 tbsp	19	tr	tr
hot dog	1 tbsp	14	tr	tr
piccalilli	1.4 oz	13	—	tr
sweet	1 tbsp	19	tr	tr
RHUBARB				
frzn, as prep w/ sugar	½ cup	139	—	tr
RICE				
brown long-grain, cooked	½ cup	109	tr	tr
glutinous, cooked	½ cup	116	tr	tr
long-grain instant, cooked	½ cup	80	tr	tr
long-grain parboiled, cooked	½ cup	100	tr	tr
pilaf	½ cup	84	1	3
risotto	6.6 oz	426	—	18
spanish	¾ cup	363	10	27
Budget Gourmet Oriental Rice With Vegetables	1 pkg (5.75 oz)	230	—	12
Knorr Risotto With Mushrooms	½ cup	110	—	tr
La Choy Chinese Fried Rice	¾ cup	190	tr	1
Lipton Golden Saute Fried Rice Chicken	½ cup	129	—	2
Lipton Rice And Sauce Beef	½ cup	119	—	1
Mahatma Jambalaya	1 cup (2 oz)	190	0	1
Minute Microwave Cheddar Cheese Broccoli	½ cup	164	2	5
Near East Lentil Pilaf, as prep w/ butter	¾ cup (4.9 oz)	180	0	1

FOOD	PORTION	CALS.	SAT. FAT	TOTAL FAT
Old El Paso Spanish	½ cup	70	0	1
Rice-A-Roni Chicken & Mushroom	½ cup	180	—	7
Success Brown & Wild	½ cup	190	0	1
Superfino Arborio Rice	½ cup	100	—	0
Uncle Ben Boil-In-Bag	1 serv (0.9 oz)	94	—	tr
Uncle Ben Country Inn Broccoli And White Cheddar	1 serv (1.2 oz)	131	—	3
RICE CAKES				
Hain 5-Grain	1	40	—	tr
Ka-Me Cheese	16 pieces (1 oz)	120	0	2
Lundberg Organic Lightly Salted	1	60	—	1
Pritikin Plain	1	35	0	0
ROLL				
cinnamon raisin	1 (2¾ in)	223	3	10
egg	1 (2½ in)	107	1	2
hard	1 (3½ in)	167	tr	2
hot cross bun	1	202	—	4
Arnold Deli Kaiser	1	170	—	2
Arnold Hamburger	1	120	—	2
August Bros. Dinner	1	90	—	1
Bread Du Jour Rye	1 (1.2 oz)	90	0	2
Bread Du Jour Sourdough	1 (2.2 oz)	140	0	2
Martin's Hoagie	1	240	—	3
Pepperidge Farm Finger Poppy Seed	1	50	0	2
Pepperidge Farm Frankfurter	1	140	1	3
Pepperidge Farm Parker House	1	60	0	1
Pillsbury Crescent	1	100	1	6
Roman Meal Brown & Serve	2 (2 oz)	140	tr	3
ROUGHY				
orange, baked	3 oz	75	tr	1
RUTABAGA				
fresh, cooked & mashed	½ cup	41	tr	tr
SABLEFISH				
smoked	1 oz	72	1	6

FOOD	PORTION	CALS.	SAT. FAT	TOTAL FAT
SALAD				
chef w/o dressing	1½ cups	386	13	28
tossed w/o dressing	1½ cups	32	0	tr
tossed w/o dressing w/ chicken	1½ cups	105	tr	2
tossed w/o dressing w/ pasta & seafood	1½ cups (14.6 oz)	380	3	21
waldorf	½ cup	79	2	6
Dole Caesar Salad	⅓ pkg (3.5 oz)	170	2	14
Dole Salad-In-A-Minute Spinach	3.5 oz	180	2	9
Fresh Express European Mix	1½ cups (3 oz)	20	0	0
Fresh Express Garden Salad	1½ cups (3 oz)	20	0	0
SALAD DRESSING				
Catalina	1 tbsp	15	0	1
Healthy Sensation French	1 tbsp	21	tr	1
Hollywood Caesar	1 tbsp	70	1	7
Kraft Blue Cheese Chunky	1 tbsp	60	1	6
Kraft Buttermilk Creamy	1 tbsp	80	1	8
Kraft Free Nonfat French	1 tbsp	26	0	0
Kraft Reduced Calorie Buttermilk Creamy	1 tbsp	30	0	3
Newman's Own Light Italian	1 tbsp (0.5 fl oz)	10	tr	tr
Pritikin Vinaigrette	1 tbsp	10	—	0
Rancher's Choice	1 tbsp	90	1	6
Roka Blue Cheese	1 tbsp	60	1	6
Roka Blue Cheese Reduced Calorie	1 tbsp	15	1	1
S&W Low Calorie Creamy Italian	1 tbsp	10	—	1
S&W No-Oil Italian	1 tbsp	2	0	0
Seven Seas Free Nonfat Red Wine Vinegar	1 tbsp	6	0	0
Seven Seas Light Thousand Island!	1 tbsp	30	0	2
Seven Seas Thousand Island Creamy	1 tbsp	50	1	5
Seven Seas Viva Light Ranch!	1 tbsp	50	1	5
Ultra Slim-Fast French	1 tbsp	20	—	tr
Walden Farms Thousand Island	1 tbsp	24	tr	2

FOOD	PORTION	CALS.	SAT. FAT	TOTAL FAT
Weight Watchers Russian	1 tbsp	50	1	5
Wishbone Classic Light Dijon Vinaigrette	1 tbsp	30	—	3
Wishbone Italian Creamy	1 tbsp	54	1	6
Wishbone Lite Creamy Italian	1 tbsp	26	tr	2
SALMON				
pink baked	3 oz	127	1	4
salmon cake	1 (3 oz)	241	7	15
Bumble Bee Pink	3.5 oz	160	2	8
Bumble Bee Red	3.5 oz	180	2	10
SALSA				
Chi-Chi's Hot Chi-Chi	2 tbsp (1 oz)	10	0	0
Frito Lay Medium	1 oz	12	0	0
Hain Mild	¼ cup	20	0	0
Hot Cha Cha Medium	2 tbsp (1 oz)	5	0	0
Newman's Own Bandito Hot	1 tbsp (0.7 oz)	6	—	tr
Old El Paso Picante Mild	2 tbsp	10	—	tr
Ortega Mild Green Chili	1 tbsp	8	0	0
Pace Thick & Chunky	2 tbsp (1 fl oz)	12	0	0
Rosarita Chunky Hot	3 tbsp (1.5 oz)	25	—	tr
SARDINES				
Empress Skinless & Boneless In Soy Oil	1 can (4.4 oz)	500	—	45
Port Clyde In Louisiana Hot Sauce	1 can (3.75 oz)	170	2	9
Underwood In Mustard Sauce	3.75 oz	220	—	16
Underwood In Tomato Sauce	3.75 oz	220	—	16
Vikings Delight Brisling In Olive Oil, drained	1 can (3.75 oz)	260	—	20
SAUCE				
barbecue	1 cup	188	1	5
teriyaki	1 tbsp	15	0	0
Best Foods Tartar	1 tbsp (14 g)	70	1	8
Heinz Worcestershire	1 tbsp	6	0	0
Heluva Good Cheese Cocktail	¼ cup (1.6 oz)	40	0	0
Hormel Not-So-Sloppy-Joe Sauce	¼ cup (2.2 oz)	70	0	0
House of Tsang Hoisin	1 tsp (6 g)	15	0	0

FOOD	PORTION	CALS.	SAT. FAT	TOTAL FAT
Ka-Me Duck Sauce	2 tbsp (1 oz)	80	0	0
Ka-Me Tamari	1 tbsp (0.5 fl oz)	10	0	1
Kikkoman Sweet & Sour	1 tbsp	19	—	tr
Lea & Perrins Steak	1 oz	40	—	tr
McIlhenny Tabasco	1 tsp	1	tr	tr
Old El Paso Enchilada Mild	¼ cup	25	—	1
Old El Paso Taco Mild	2 tbsp	10	—	tr
Pace Picante	2 tbsp (1 fl oz)	7	0	0
Progresso Alfredo	½ cup	340	19	30
Progresso Primavera Creamy	½ cup	190	10	17

SAUERKRAUT

fresh	½ cup	22	tr	tr

SAUERKRAUT JUICE

S&W	4 oz	14	0	0

SAUSAGE

bratwurst pork	3 oz	256	8	22
italian, cooked	1 (3 oz)	268	8	21
kielbasa pork	2 oz	176	6	16
knockwurst	3 oz	261	8	24
pork, cooked	1 link (1 oz)	96	2	8
vienna, canned	1 (½ oz)	45	1	4
Brown & Serve Beef	1	90	—	9
Brown & Serve Light	1	60	—	5
Hillshire Links Cheddarwurst Lite	1 link (2.7 oz)	190	—	15
Jones Scrapple	1 slice (1½ oz)	90	—	6
Louis Rich Turkey	2.5 oz	110	3	6
Perdue Breakfast Patties Turkey, cooked	1 (1.3 oz)	61	1	4

SAUSAGE DISHES

sausage roll	1 (4.6 oz)	622	—	48
Jimmy Dean Microwave Sausage Biscuits	1	210	—	14

SAUSAGE SUBSTITUTES

Morningstar Farms Breakfast Links	2 (45 g)	90	—	5

FOOD	PORTION	CALS.	SAT. FAT	TOTAL FAT
SCALLOP				
breaded & fried	2 lg	67	1	3
SCONE				
fruit	1 (1.75 oz)	158	—	5
plain	1 (1.75 oz)	181	—	7
SCUP				
baked	3 oz	115	—	3
SEAWEED				
kombu	1 oz	12	tr	tr
nori	1 oz	10	tr	tr
SESAME				
seeds dried	1 tbsp	52	1	5
Sesame Tahini Arrowhead	1 oz	170	—	17
SHAD				
baked	3 oz	214	—	15
roe, baked w/ butter & lemon	3.5 oz	126	—	3
SHALLOTS				
raw, chopped	1 tbsp	7	tr	tr
SHELLFISH SUBSTITUTES				
surimi	1 oz	28	—	tr
Louis Kemp Crab Delights Chunk Style	2 oz	54	—	tr
SHELLIE BEANS				
canned	½ cup	37	tr	tr
SHERBET				
Borden Orange	½ cup	110	—	1
Sealtest Lime	½ cup (3 oz)	130	0	1
SHRIMP				
breaded & fried	4 large	73	1	4
canned	1 cup	154	tr	3
cooked	4 large	22	tr	tr
Microwave Entree Shrimp Scampi Gorton's	1 pkg	390	—	30
SMELT				
cooked	3 oz	106	tr	3

FOOD	PORTION	CALS.	SAT. FAT	TOTAL FAT
SNACKS				
Bugles	1 oz	150	—	8
Cheetos Crunchy	26 pieces (1 oz)	150	—	9
Cheez Doodles Puffed	1 oz	150	—	9
Chex Snack Mix Traditional Chex	⅔ cup (1.2 oz)	150	1	5
Combos Cheddar	1 pkg (1.7 oz)	250	3	13
Cornnuts Original	1 pkg (2 oz)	260	2	8
Doo Dads	1 oz	130	1	6
Funyums Onion Rings	11 pieces (1 oz)	140	—	7
Hain Carrot Chips	1 oz	150	—	9
Lance Pork Skins	1 pkg (14 g)	80	2	5
Ultra Slim-Fast Lite N' Tasty Cheese Curls	1 oz	110	—	3
Weight Watchers Apple Chips	¾ oz	70	0	0
Weight Watchers Cheese Curls	½ oz	70	1	2
SNAIL				
raw	3 oz	117	tr	tr
SNAPPER				
cooked	3 oz	109	tr	1
SODA				
cream	12 oz	191	0	0
quinine	12 oz	125	0	0
Canada Dry Seltzer	8 fl oz	0	0	0
Canada Dry Ginger Ale	8 fl oz	100	0	0
Canada Dry Tonic Water Diet	8 fl oz	0	0	0
Clearly Canadian	8 fl oz	0	0	0
Clearly Canadian Black Cherry	8 fl oz	2	—	0
Coca-Cola Cherry	8 fl oz	104	0	0
Coca-Cola Classic	8 fl oz	97	0	0
Crush Orange	8 fl oz	140	0	0
Diet Coke	8 fl oz	1	0	0
Diet Pepsi	8 fl oz	1	0	0
Diet Rite Cola	8 fl oz	1	0	0
Dr Pepper	1 oz	13	—	0
Fresca	8 fl oz	3	0	0
Hires Root Beer	8 fl oz	130	0	0

FOOD	PORTION	CALS.	SAT. FAT	TOTAL FAT
Orangina	6 fl oz	80	0	0
Pepsi-Cola	8 fl oz	105	0	0
7 Up	1 oz	12	—	0
Sprite	8 fl oz	100	0	0
Welch's Sparkling Grape	12 oz	180	—	0
Yoo-Hoo	9 fl oz	150	tr	tr
SOLE				
battered & fried	3.2 oz	211	3	11
fresh, cooked	1 fillet (4.5 oz)	148	tr	2
SOUP				
asparagus cream of, as prep w/ milk	1 cup	161	3	8
beef broth ready-to-serve	1 can (14 oz)	27	tr	1
black bean turtle soup	1 cup	218	tr	1
chicken broth, as prep w/ water	1 cup	39	tr	1
chicken noodle, as prep w/ water	1 cup	75	1	2
clam chowder Manhattan, as prep w/ water	1 cup	77	tr	2
clam chowder New England, as prep w/ milk	1 cup	163	3	7
escarole ready-to-serve	1 cup	27	1	2
french onion, as prep w/ water	1 cup	57	tr	2
gazpacho ready-to-serve	1 cup	57	tr	2
minestrone, as prep w/ water	1 cup	83	1	3
mushroom cream of, as prep w/ water	1 cup	129	2	9
split pea w/ ham, as prep w/ water	1 cup	189	2	4
tomato, as prep w/ milk	1 cup	160	3	6
vegetarian vegetable, as prep w/ water	1 cup	72	tr	2
vichyssoise	1 cup	148	4	6
Campbell Won Ton	8 oz	40	—	1
Cup-A-Ramen Oriental With Vegetables Low Fat, as prep	8 oz	220	—	2
Gold's Borscht	8 oz	100	0	0
Gold's Borscht Lo-Cal	8 oz	20	—	tr

FOOD	PORTION	CALS.	SAT. FAT	TOTAL FAT
Goodman's Matzo Ball Soup	1 cup	40	0	1
Maruchan Instant Lunch Oriental Noodles Beef	1 pkg (2.25 oz)	290	—	13
Maruchan Instant Lunch Oriental Noodles Mushroom	1 pkg (2.25 oz)	290	—	13
Maruchan Instant Lunch Oriental Noodles Shrimp	1 pkg (2.25 oz)	290	—	13
SOUR CREAM				
Sealtest	1 tbsp	30	2	3
Sealtest Light Cultured Half & Half	1 tbsp	25	1	2
SOUR CREAM SUBSTITUTES				
Better Than Sour Cream Sour Supreme Tofutti	1 oz	50	2	5
SOY				
soy milk	1 cup	79	1	5
soybean sprouts, stir fried	1 cup	125	1	7
soybeans, cooked	1 cup	298	2	15
soybeans salted, roasted & toasted	1 oz	129	1	7
Lightlife Tempeh	4 oz	182	1	6
SOY SAUCE				
La Choy	½ tsp	2	—	tr
La Choy Lite	½ tsp	1	—	tr
SPAGHETTI SAUCE				
Classico Beef & Pork	4 fl oz	80	—	4
Contadina	¼ cup	20	0	0
Contadina Alfredo	½ cup (4.2 fl oz)	400	21	38
Contadina Light Alfredo	½ cup (4.2 fl oz)	190	7	13
Contadina Light Garden Vegetable	½ cup (4.4 fl oz)	45	0	1
Contadina Pesto With Basil	¼ cup (2 oz)	310	5	30
Healthy Choice Extra Chunky Garlic & Onions	½ cup (4.4 oz)	50	0	1
Hunt's Classic Italian With Parmesan	½ cup (4.4 fl oz)	50	0	2
Newman's Own Marinara	4 oz	70	—	2

FOOD	PORTION	CALS.	SAT. FAT	TOTAL FAT
Prego Chunky Sausage & Green Peppers	4 oz	160	—	8
Progresso Bolognese	½ cup	150	2	12
Ragu Fino Italian Sliced Mushroom	½ cup (4.5 oz)	90	0	3
Weight Watchers With Meat	⅓ cup	45	0	1
SPANISH FOOD				
burrito w/ beans	2 (7.6 oz)	448	7	14
burrito w/ beans, cheese & beef	2 (7.1 oz)	331	7	13
chimichanga w/ beef	1 (6.1 oz)	425	9	20
enchilada w/ cheese & beef	1 (6.7 oz)	324	9	18
enchirito w/ cheese, beef & beans	1 (6.8 oz)	344	8	16
frijoles w/ cheese	1 cup (5.9 oz)	226	4	8
nachos w/ cheese & jalapeno peppers	6 to 8 (7.2 oz)	607	14	34
taco	1 sm (6 oz)	370	11	21
taco salad	1½ cups	279	7	15
tostada w/ guacamole	2 (9.2 oz)	360	10	23
Derby Tamales	2	160	3	7
Gebhardt Enchiladas	2	310	9	24
Gebhardt Taco Shell	1	50	2	2
Old El Paso Menudo	½ can	476	21	52
SPINACH				
canned	½ cup	25	tr	1
fresh, cooked	½ cup	21	tr	tr
frzn, cooked	½ cup	27	tr	tr
raw, chopped	½ cup	6	tr	tr
Stouffer's Creamed	½ cup (2.25 oz)	150	4	12
SPINACH JUICE				
spinach juice	3½ oz	7	0	0
SPORTS DRINKS				
Gatorade	1 cup (8 fl oz)	50	0	0
PowerAde Lemon-Lime	8 fl oz	72	0	0
Slice All Sport Punch	8 fl oz	81	0	0
SQUASH				
acorn, cubed & baked	½ cup	57	tr	tr

FOOD	PORTION	CALS.	SAT. FAT	TOTAL FAT
butternut, baked	½ cup	41	tr	tr
spaghetti, cooked	½ cup	23	tr	tr
SQUID				
fried	3 oz	149	2	6
STRAWBERRIES				
fresh	1 cup	45	tr	1
whole sweetened frzn	1 cup	200	tr	tr
STRAWBERRY JUICE				
Kool-Aid Koolers	1 (8.45 oz)	136	0	0
Kern's Nectar	6 fl oz	110	0	0
STUFFING/DRESSING				
bread, as prep w/ water & fat	½ cup	251	6	15
Stove Top Chicken, as prep	½ cup	176	tr	8
Stove Top Cornbread, as prep	½ cup	175	—	8
Stove Top Flex Serve Homestyle Herb, as prep	½ cup	173	—	9
STURGEON				
smoked	1 oz	48	tr	1
SUGAR				
white	1 packet (6 g)	25	0	0
Hollywood Turbinado	1 tbsp	50	0	0
SUGAR SUBSTITUTES				
Equal	1 pkg	4	0	0
Sweet One	1 pkg (1 g)	4	0	0
SUNFLOWER SEEDS				
toasted & salted	1 oz	176	2	16
SUSHI				
california roll	1 piece (0.8 oz)	28	tr	1
kim chi	⅓ cup (5.8 oz)	18	tr	tr
sashimi	1 serv (6 oz)	198	1	7
tuna roll	1 piece (0.7 oz)	23	tr	tr
vegetable roll	1 piece (1.2 oz)	27	tr	1
vinegared ginger	⅓ cup (1.6 oz)	48	tr	tr
wasabi	2 tsp (0.3 oz)	5	0	tr
yellowtail roll	1 piece (0.6 oz)	25	tr	1

FOOD	PORTION	CALS.	SAT. FAT	TOTAL FAT
SWEET POTATO				
baked w/ skin	1 (3½ oz)	118	tr	tr
canned in syrup	½ cup	106	tr	tr
Royal Prince Candied	½ cup (4.9 oz)	210	0	1
SWEETBREADS				
beef, braised	3 oz	230	—	15
SWISS CHARD				
fresh, cooked	½ cup	18	—	tr
SWORDFISH				
cooked	3 oz	132	1	4
SYRUP				
Home Brands Maple	1 oz	110	—	0
Smucker's Fruit Syrup All Flavors	2 tbsp	100	0	0
TANGERINE				
fresh	1	37	tr	tr
TANGERINE JUICE				
Minute Maid frzn	8 fl oz	120	0	0
TARO				
chips	10 (0.8 oz)	115	1	6
TEA/HERBAL TEA				
brewed tea	6 oz	2	0	0
Bigelow Chamomile	5 fl oz	tr	—	tr
Bigelow Hibiscus & Rose Hips	5 fl oz	1	—	tr
Bigelow Peppermint	5 fl oz	tr	—	tr
Celestial Seasonings Ginseng Plus	8 fl oz	3	—	tr
Celestial Seasonings Lemon Zinger	8 fl oz	4	—	tr
TEMPEH				
tempeh	½ cup	165	1	6
TILEFISH				
cooked	3 oz	125	1	4
TOFU				
firm	¼ block (3 oz)	118	1	7
fresh, fried	1 piece (½ oz)	35	tr	3
regular	¼ block (4 oz)	88	1	6

FOOD	PORTION	CALS.	SAT. FAT	TOTAL FAT
TOFU YOGURT				
Stir Fruity Strawberry	6 oz	140	—	2
TOMATILLO				
fresh, chopped	½ cup	21	—	1
TOMATO				
red	1 (4½ oz)	2	tr	tr
sauce spanish style	½ cup	40	tr	tr
sun dried	1 piece	5	tr	tr
sun dried in oil	1 piece (3 g)	6	tr	tr
w/ green chiles	½ cup	18	tr	tr
Contadina Crushed	¼ cup	20	0	0
Contadina Pasta Ready Tomatoes	½ cup	50	0	2
Hebrew National Pickled	⅓ tomato (1 oz)	4	0	0
Hunt's Paste	1 oz	25	0	0
TOMATO JUICE				
Libby's	6 oz	35	0	0
TORTILLA				
Mariachi	1	112	—	3
TROUT				
baked	3 oz	162	1	7
TUNA				
fresh, cooked	3 oz	157	1	5
Bumble Bee Chunk Light In Water	2 oz	60	1	1
S&W Chunk Light Fancy In Oil	2 oz	140	—	10
TUNA DISHES				
tuna salad	1 cup	383	3	19
tuna salad submarine sandwich w/ lettuce & oil	1	584	5	28
TURBOT				
baked	3 oz	104	—	3
TURKEY				
bologna	1 oz	57	—	4
breast	1 slice (¾ oz)	23	tr	tr
breast w/ skin, roasted	4 oz	212	2	8
dark meat w/ skin, roasted	3.6 oz	230	4	12

FOOD	PORTION	CALS.	SAT. FAT	TOTAL FAT
ground, cooked	3 oz	188	3	11
pastrami	2 oz	80	1	4
salami, cooked	2 oz	111	—	8
Carl Buddig	1 oz	50	1	3
TURNIPS				
canned greens	½ cup	17	tr	tr
cooked, mashed	½ cup (4.2 oz)	47	tr	tr
fresh greens chopped, cooked	½ cup	15	tr	tr
VEAL				
cutlet lean only, fried	3 oz	156	1	4
ground, broiled	3 oz	146	3	6
loin chop w/ bone lean & fat, braised	1 chop (2.8 oz)	227	5	14
VEAL DISHES				
parmigiana	4.2 oz	279	10	18
VEGETABLE JUICE				
V8	6 fl oz	35	—	0
VEGETABLES MIXED				
caponata	¼ cup	28	—	1
mixed vegetables	½ cup	39	tr	tr
pakoras	1 (2 oz)	108	—	5
peas & carrots	½ cup	48	tr	tr
peas & onions	½ cup	40	tr	tr
ratatouille	8.8 oz	190	—	16
samosa	2 (4 oz)	519	—	46
succotash	½ cup	79	tr	1
VENISON				
roasted	3 oz	134	1	3
WAFFLES				
plain	1 (7 in diam)	218	2	11
WALNUTS				
english, dried	1 oz	182	2	18
WATER CHESTNUTS				
chinese, sliced	½ cup	35	—	tr

1 oz. Walnuts = ¼ C.

FOOD	PORTION	CALS.	SAT. FAT	TOTAL FAT
WATERCRESS				
raw, chopped	½ cup	2	tr	tr
WATERMELON				
cut up	1 cup	50	—	1
wedge	1/16	152	—	2
WHEAT GERM				
Kretschmer	¼ cup	103	1	3
WHIPPED TOPPINGS				
Cool Whip Extra Creamy	1 tbsp	13	—	1
Kraft Whipped Topping	¼ cup	35	3	3
WHITE BEANS				
canned	1 cup	306	tr	1
dried, cooked	1 cup	249	tr	1
WHITEFISH				
smoked	1 oz	39	tr	tr
WILD RICE				
cooked	½ cup	83	tr	tr
WINE				
Boone's Sangria	1 fl oz	22	0	0
Carlo Rossi Burgundy	1 fl oz	22	0	0
Carlo Rossi Chablis	1 fl oz	21	0	0
Fairbanks Cream Sherry	1 fl oz	42	0	0
Fairbanks Port	1 fl oz	44	0	0
Gallo Cabernet Sauvignon	1 fl oz	22	0	0
Gallo Red Rosé	1 fl oz	23	0	0
WINE COOLERS				
Bartles & Jaymes Original	12 fl oz	190	0	0
YAM				
cubed, cooked	½ cup	79	tr	tr
YEAST				
brewer's dry	1 tbsp	25	tr	tr
YOGURT				
Breyers Lowfat Strawberry	8 oz	250	1	2
Breyers Lowfat Vanilla Bean	8 oz	230	2	3
Colombo Fat Free Apricot	8 oz	190	0	0

FOOD	PORTION	CALS.	SAT. FAT	TOTAL FAT
Colombo Fat Free Plain	8 oz	110	0	0
Colombo Fat Free Strawberry	8 oz	190	0	0
Colombo Fat Free Vanilla	8 oz	170	0	0
Colombo Low Fat Plain	8 oz	120	3	5
Dannon Nonfat Light Cherry Vanilla	8 oz	100	—	0
Dannon Nonfat Strawberry	6 oz	140	—	0
Friendship Fruit Crunch Strawberry	6 oz	190	2	5
Yoplait Custard Style Blueberry	6 oz	190	—	4
Yoplait Original Plain	6 oz	130	—	3
Yoplait Original Vanilla	6 oz	180	—	3
YOGURT FROZEN				
Ben & Jerry's Chocolate	½ cup (4 fl oz)	140	2	3
Borden Strawberry	½ cup	100	—	2
Elan Coffee	4 oz	130	—	3
Haagen-Dazs Vanilla	3 oz	130	2	3
ZUCCHINI				
raw, sliced	½ cup	9	tr	tr
sliced, cooked	½ cup	14	tr	tr
Progresso Italian Style	½ cup	50	tr	2